THE RE-CREATION OF EVE

ROSEMARY HAUGHTON

TEMPLEGATE PUBLISHERS
Springfield, Illinois

ACKNOWLEDGEMENTS

This book came into existence with much help, and I want to thank especially Ruth, who typed it from my hieroglyphics, and Carol who helped to decipher them, for their patient labour of friendship. I want to thank the Wellspring community for the support and understanding which enabled me to take time to write among all the demands of a home serving women especially, and for the inspiration of their example of active and healing care for people very like those in this book. Most of all I am grateful to Nancy, who thrashed out ideas with me, challenged and affirmed me, in the long process of making a book.

CONTENTS

Made and printed in the United States by

Templegate Publishers
302 East Adams St./P.O. Box 5152
Springfield, Illinois 62705

ISBN 0-87243-135-5

INTRODUCTION

We live in a time when the struggle of women for their rights in church and society is part of a great movement of liberation of all kinds of oppressed people in every part of our world. The movement, if it is to 'succeed' and become the seed of a future world of justice and peace, is not about those who have been the oppressed overcoming the oppressors, claiming their goods and positions, continuing the oppressive structures. That would be to do again what has been done repeatedly throughout history — the liberated oppressed become the new oppressors. Those who proclaim freedom must do so not only in words, but also in actions, and most importantly by imagining and creating structures for church and society appropriate to the vision of justice and peace.

Our challenge as human beings responsible for the life of a planet on the brink of destruction is to be very much in touch with the realities of our world, to act out of our awareness, to reflect on the appropriateness and effectiveness of our actions, and then to act again. The process of on-going reflection is essential if we are to be faithful to the vision which inspires our direction and action. We bring to reflection not only our personal and communal experiences and an understanding of the realities of our world, but also a critical sense of history and tradition. For Christians this requires a profound understanding of scripture.

This is why this book by Rosemary is timely and important. It is a valuable source for evaluating and validating the contemporary experience of Christian women. This book is one more of the many which have been written in the last decade to explore the experience of women in the church, from the time of Jesus until now, and part of Rosemary's research for this book involved reading many of these. But as those of us who have read her previous works would expect, her approach is somewhat different. Rosemary makes full use of biblical scholarship, but she also looks to human experience as the place of God's revelation and she is compelled to search for the human experiences which are at the heart of the gospel stories which she explores in this book. She does what each of us as a Christian is called to do — to read and study and pray scripture in such a way that it challenges and enlarges our own experience of being human. Rosemary's methodology requires us to use our imaginations, as well as our reason, and in doing so, to enter the human experience of Jesus' interaction with people of his times, people not unlike those who today are regarded as marginal and unimportant by the power structures of society.

It is important to say something about the circumstances in which this book was written because it demonstrates the kind of reflection in which there is an interplay between the experiences of contemporary women and the experiences of the 'women with Jesus' and those in the young church. Rosemary has been for three years a member of Wellspring House, the home of an ecumenical Christian community in Gloucester, Ma. Wellspring is a house of hospitality for homeless people and the base for Movement for North American Mission, a training program for lay people who feel called to serve the poor of North America. The majority of guests who stay at Wellspring are women, women who have suffered abuse of every kind and who are often labelled as the failures of society because of life-styles they have chosen as means of survival. They are not unlike the prostitutes, the adultresses, the desperate women with sick children whom Jesus encountered and to whose need and pain he responded with openness and deep compassion.

'The Re-creation of Eve' was written in the midst of interacting with these kinds of women, listening to their hopes for a different kind of life and helping them to take the first steps to achieve them. The book was also written as the Wellspring community reflected on our shared ministry and tried to discover meaning in experiences which often involved apparent failure, much conflict, frustration and pain. Again and again our touchstone has been the centrality of the liberation of women in the ministry of Jesus, in which he proclaimed in word and deed the possibility of a different kind of social reality where people live as friends — cooperatively, mutually, and interdependently.

Faith in the possibility of a different kind of world is the common vision of the women and men who are now part of Movement for North American Mission, of which Rosemary is co-director. It is true for this small movement, like many others in the church today, that there are more women than men who take part in the training — women who are in touch with the calling and power given to them by Jesus and who are discovering new ways to live that out in structures which are appropriate to the vision of a just and free world. Rosemary's book is important for those who are engaged in this enterprise because it is about our 'ancestors' who are also our sisters, the women whom Jesus affirmed as disciples and the women of the young church who knew themselves as called and empowered for ministry in which the categories of sex, nationality, and social status made no sense. Knowing and telling the stories of our heritage is a vital part of the process of reclaiming our 'birthright' as women and of living the privileges of that with fidelity.

It seems that this is the unique time in history when women and men have the possibility to unleash again the feminine energy at work in the core of the cosmos — the energy with which Jesus was so passionately in touch. We have the historical hindsight to understand how it was blocked in the history of the church and what that loss meant for humanity. We have the scientific and psychological insight to understand the need for it and how essential it is for personal and social growth and transformation. And we have the groaning of a desperately sick and endangered world calling us to respond urgently for the sake of the survival of humanity. This calling is at the heart of Christian ministry which Rosemary discloses in her book. It is the ministry she has lived in her family and with her friends in community. As her friend I am grateful to share in her life and work, lived out of deep faith in the possibility of a transformed world.

— by Nancy Schwoyer

FOREWORD

The first woman, as Hebrew tradition explains her, is of a like nature with the man, and with him makes up the human thing. But in the other version of the creation story she is, though of like nature, created explicitly to support and complement the man. And the story of the fall of humankind, and the punishment for it, lays on the woman a penalty of subjugation and suffering as wife and mother. Eve, as she is then called, stands as the explanation and justification of the subjugation of women in a patriarchal society.

There are vestiges and hints of times and places when women were not secondary, not possessions of the male, but fully human, even dominant. The earth mother and all the ancient goddesses on whom life and growth depended, reflected in their theology and their rites the reverence for the life-bearing power of women. But the vestiges are hard to uncover, the hints are ambiguous, for the great patriarchal cultures have made it their business to eliminate all traces of a worship which validated the claim of women to power and influence. The Christian fathers were equally diligent in this matter, and they had a hard fight for they had to combat the remaining goddess cults of Greece, Rome and Egypt — Aphrodite/Diana, and the great Isis, and later the northern "old religion" of the Celts, with its fertility rites, which eventually went underground and survived to become "witchcraft." But the official church, by then busy justifying its own patriarchal structure as inevitable and God-given, had also to work hard to eliminate the power of women who were Christians, and that was more difficult, because something had happened to women around Jesus which did not fit the expectations of the male-dominated cultures. Yet it could not be allowed that women should have leadership or even equal status in the Christian church as it grew and accommodated itself to the surrounding culture. Eve came in very useful — Eve, the symbol of women's innate sinfulness, her power to degrade and corrupt, or a symbol of divine punishment laid on all womankind.

The job of suppressing women in Christianity turned out to be very difficult. No matter how much it was theologically justified, shown to be a part of the nature of things, and ordained by God, women kept on displaying powers they were not supposed to have, engaging in prophecy and ministry of which they were not supposed to be capable.

They were threatened, harrassed, vilified, made to do penance, beaten, tortured and even burned as witches. Yet it kept on happening. These women who felt the power of God and responded were not pagan, they did not invoke the goddess, they called on Christ and claimed Jesus as their justification. They were convinced, against all kinds of emotional pressures and spiritual blackmail, that they were indeed called and spirit-guided. They were, in some sense, claiming their heritage as God's creation, as the daughters of an Eve who was not the source of sin but of life. But they knew this not in the rejection of Christianity but by their awareness of the very heart of the Christian tradition, in which was proclaimed liberty to captives, freedom for the oppressed, love and acceptance and blessing for the weakest and most downtrodden.

Many of the women throughout history who resisted the pressures of patriarchy (though they didn't call it that, or even reject all its claims) referred explicitly to the women of the New Testament as their inspiration and justification — the women who first carried news of the Resurrection, who were faithful when the men were faithless. Their arguments were rejected with long explanations, but they would not disappear. These women knew deeply, even though they could seldom spell it out consciously, that they were being denied their birthright. They struggled to affirm the calling and power given to women by Jesus, who had recreated the image of womenhood when he called all people into a different relationship. It was as if woman and man and child, beast and bird, fish and foliage, were re-created according to the nature which is theirs at the heart of the divine experience.

For whatever marvels are told of Jesus of Nazareth, this was the marvel beyond all others: that he was able to call Eve out of the kingdom of shades, and greet her in the garden of a renewed Eden, outside the tomb to which a patriarchal culture had relegated him. The hold of such a culture is not a superficial, temporary grip; it is as deep in each person as their own personhood; it determines the direction and the description; it sets the limits and the goals; it separates right from wrong and high from low, man from woman, ruler from subject, and defines the status of each with all the power of a great myth. To have broken that spell, to have given to those bound by it the freedom to let it all go, and walk free and powerful, was a wonder of healing unequalled. That is why, at this time in human history, it is necessary to recognize that it was done, that it was never altogether contained or suppressed, and that now it can be claimed and proclaimed as the essential salvation of a culture which has decided to doom itself to death, because it has so feared life. It is time to try to understand what happened to those first women who encountered the prophet from Nazareth, and were transformed, and transformed others.

This is not, on the face of it, a very novel notion. There must be dozens of books about biblical women, some better than others, and many with considerable depth and power of inspiration. Until recently, however, the only way such accounts of biblical women could be written was within the context assigned to women by the patriarchal culture in which they lived and in which the writers lived. It was assumed by the writers, men or women, that the greatness of these women consisted either in the devotion, compassion and skill they brought to the feminine role which they accepted, or in the way in which they responded to circumstances which demanded that they abandon briefly the proper feminine role.

Judith, the Jewish national heroine for her slaying of the enemy general, was acclaimed for saving her people, but certainly not regarded as a fitting model for womanhood in general. The wives of the patriarchs, Sarah, Rebecca, Rachel, were acclaimed for their obedience rather than their enterprise, and Miriam, prophetess and leader, was struck with leprosy for being too forward. In the New Testament, Mary of Nazareth has notoriously been presented as weak, retiring and quiet, the warrior maiden of the *Magnificat* quite cancelled out by the need for a suitable role model for women under patriarchy. More subtly she becomes the supreme symbol of the feminine role, that of the redemptive power of silent acceptance and suffering. Mary Magdalen, dynamic and irrepressible, was identified with the weeping sinner, and her calling as prophet of resurrection overlaid by the image of the redeemed but ever prostrate penitent, clinging and romantically grieving. Dorcas has become simply a symbol for the pious seamstress of the "Dorcas Circles," sewing for the poor, and nobody enquires why the community she lived in felt her death to be an unbearable loss. So the women of the "New Covenant" are processed into the same patriarchal mould as their foremothers, acclaimed for characteristics which they did not exhibit, at least as far as the records allow us to reconstruct them. The memory of them is made to fit the requirements of a religious system which has decided that women must forever occupy a subordinate role; their glory is a reflected glory as they support and enhance the effective role of the men.

Yet the Christian proclamation concerns the possibility of a new people in which old categories, old oppressions, are set aside. The new Covenant is sealed in the blood of one who died because he challenged and set aside the cherished categories of church and state and announced that God made no distinctions, that the Abba he intimately knew was incapable of excluding even the weakest and worst, and who indeed had quite unacceptable notions of what was worst. He summoned disciples from all classes and specifically called on them to abandon patriarchal family loyalties in favor of the new community bonded by faith in God's promises. He sent out his followers to proclaim this new reality and live it.

The record of obedience to his commands is not impressive. It took a long time for Christians to reject slavery, even longer for them to learn respect for people of other cultures; the class system was blessed by the churches for most of the Christian centuries, and the use of war as a method of settling differences has seldom been seriously questioned by official Christianity until nuclear weapons forced the issue. Yet in all these areas there has been change, there has been a recognition of failure and a desire to respond to the challenge.

The area in which it has been most difficult for Christianity to recognize, let alone respond to, the challenge of what Jesus did and said is that of the role of women. The radical change he demanded in that area was so difficult for a patriarchal society to deal with that it was, from the beginning, a source of friction, and it was not long before it began to be explained away. The history of women as full members of the new people Jesus called for was, as we can now see, merely a brief hiccup in the relentless rhetoric of patriarchy.

That rhetoric is being questioned and contradicted, its weaknesses exposed from within and without. The vast cultural superstructure which it legitimizes is shaken by the very success of its own logic carried to the extreme we now experience. Men and women question and reject it, seek alternatives before it is too late, and the feminist critique of our predicament calls for a new language to express a different kind of relatedness. Christians recognize that this is what Jesus himself was calling for, but it is extremely difficult to demonstrate this because of the way in which the whole Jesus story has been adapted to support, rather than challenge, the way things are. For Christian women, convinced that the gospel message is indeed the message of transformation which we need, there is constant grief in the fact that almost all the documents, liturgies, devotions and structures of Christianity are based on the assumption that the patriarchal model is the only natural one, so that all it needs is to be made kind, rather than brutal. We lack the language to express an alternative.

But language is history. Words express the experienced reality of women and men, and the reality forges the words. To discover a language we have to re-discover the history that has not been written, and to know the history we have to struggle with a language that can tell it. More and more writers are retelling history, not from the point of view of the conquerors (whose first assignment after conquest is always to re-write the history books) but from the point of view of those Jesus called the little ones — the marginal, the poor, the ones whose labour makes possible the culture of the dominant classes. Their suffering and their hopes, their art (suppressed but real) and their humor find a different language, and we are slowly learning it.

If women are to bring to this threatened world the hope of an alternative vision, offering a different way for human beings to relate to each other, they need a language in which to express it, and that means they need to know the history. The artist, Judy Chicago, wrote an introduction to the volumes which illustrate her great project in art and craft called "the Dinner Party", to which I shall be referring in a later part of this book. This exhibit is a vast triangular table, with place settings for thirty-three women from pre-history to the present, women who made a difference, each plate and runner symbolizing each woman's being and achievement. She tells how she came to design this immense work in celebration of women, and was led stage by stage to a thing of great scale and symbolic importance. Her idea, at first, grew out of a desire to celebrate in art great women of history, to create a kind of "Last Supper" at which women would be the guests. It is significant that this woman who is not a Christian should have felt challenged by the Christian symbol of table fellowship and recognized in it the essential symbolic point where bonds of acceptance, and the sharing of life, must be expressed. This idea had important implications, as Judy Chicago makes clear:

> "... The Last Supper existed within the context of the Bible, which was the history of a people. So my 'Dinner Party' would also be a people's history, the history of women in Western civilization ... I had been personally strengthened by discovering

> my rich heritage as a woman, and the enormous amount of information that existed about women's contribution to society. This information, however, was totally outside the mainstream of historical thought and was certainly unknown to most people. And as long as women's achievements were excluded from our understanding of the past we would continue to feel as if we had *never* done anything worthwhile. This absence of any sense of our tradition as women seemed to cripple us psychologically. I wanted to change that, and I wanted to do it through art."*

Christian women have a long experience of being made to feel they have "never done anything worthwhile." That is indeed a crippling experience, and it is intended to be, as much as Chinese foot-binding of women was intended to be. But at the source of our tradition is the man who told cripples to get up and walk, who was constantly telling people they were worthwhile, that they could and must do worthwhile things. He said it to women, and they heard and responded. If we are to respond to that now, to get up and walk and persuade others to walk with us, then we need to know the history of those women, to know what they were like, how they felt, what difference it made to them. To make such a discovery takes us "outside the mainstream" of theological thought. We have to be in touch with events and feelings which have been "excluded from our understanding." (And this process of exclusion has been, as more and more evidence shows, not due merely to ignorance but has involved fully deliberate suppression and even falsification of documents.) We have to enter imaginatively into an experience which utterly transformed the lives of women, yet an experience which has to be reconstructed from scanty evidence, distorted by unconscious prejudice and a lot of sheer confusion.

In this book I have attempted to touch into the transforming experience which happened to women who encountered Jesus, directly and indirectly. It has continued to happen, here and there, powerfully and constantly, but I am mainly concerned with the experience of the women we encounter in the New Testament writings themselves. The difficulties of this are obvious, and I shall be referring to them. The need for a foundation of accurate and honest scholarship is obvious too, and for this I am indebted to other women, and men, who have challenged ac-

***The Dinner Party*. A symbol of our heritage. Vol. 1. Judy Chicago, Anchor Press: Doubleday, p. 12.

cepted exegesis and done historical and textual research which opens up possibilities of different interpretation. On this basis I have tried to recover imaginatively the nature of the experience of these women, and to some extent at least this is bound to be speculative, so that the words "possibly", "maybe", "perhaps" and "probably" are appropriate. Other interpretations are possible and desirable. The important point is that we begin to identify with a human reality that was unprecedented and transforming. Nothing less can explain the things that happened, and nothing less will do for us. Unless we can understand what happened to these women, and why their experience was later undermined and set aside, we cannot bring much, as Christian women, to the ministry of hope in our time.

It is not enough for Christian women to work (with however much devotion and courage) within the categories assigned to them by a patriarchal tradition. To do that means to continue to serve the values and structures which have brought the world to the brink of destruction. We need to go back to the source, to discover the history of women as Jesus called them to be and to serve. We need to know those women as sisters, people with the limitation of their time and mentality as we are of ours, yet people capable of becoming new, and leading others to new life. The message of resurrection was entrusted to women for good reasons, as we shall see. If there is to be an announcement of life to a world rendered numb and despairing it will have to come from women, and from those men not afraid to feel with the feminine in themselves. We shall begin that work with more clarity and confidence if we can understand a little what happened to those first women: Eve re-created. We may be able to accept the mission to which they were called, in the power which empowered them.

I.
THE WOMAN WHO CAME OUT OF THE SHADOWS

A woman pushed her way through the crowd, patiently pressing herself between the bodies of the unheeding people who thronged the narrow street. Some did not notice her at all, so preoccupied were they with more important things. Others protested momentarily at her irritating and unbecoming persistence, but she was not important enough to retain anyone's attention for long. There was about her an undemanding but inflexible determination to get where she wanted to be, and she was quite accustomed to being ignored or rebuked, so the reactions of the people did not deter her. If only she could be safe from recognition! For she had no business to be in the street at all, and she did not ask for help or sympathy, which were not to be expected.

This woman stood, as she had been born, in the shadows of history where women had lived since there was history, for history was written by men. Somewhere within those shadows there surged the dim memories of a place (or was it a time, or a story inside a time or a place?) where women danced, grew tall, shaped the pattern of living. But those memories, if they were memories, survived only in the nightmares of the men who decided what were the patterns of reality. This woman stood, then, in the shadows, but she moved now to the edge of the shadows. Unknowing, driven only by obscure hope, she stood on the edge of darkness, and then took a step forward.

Her progress was slow, for the street was more than usually packed with curious and excited people who had heard, as she had, that Jesus of

Nazareth was in the town. She had waited and planned for such an opportunity ever since she had first begun to understand the significance of the stories she heard about this man, stories not only of healing but of welcome offered to the poor and outcast. It would be too much to expect that welcome could be given to such unclean creatures as herself, yet in her isolation, with little in her life to distract her from a thought once rooted in her imagination, she had brooded on those stories. In time a strange but obstinate hope began to grow until it became a fixed intention, almost an obsession, waiting only its chance. If only, unseen, she could at least touch him — perhaps — perhaps.

Yet when at last he came he was not at all at leisure, and it seemed all too likely that she would miss him, for the news she picked up from the crowd was that he was hurrying to the home of a wealthy citizen whose child was critically ill. Her chance of approaching him unseen did not seem great, but having come so far she had little to lose, indeed she had already lost all that seemed worth having. She neither expected nor wanted the conscious attention of the healer, so she pressed forward more urgently than ever, strengthened by a mixture of desperation and sheer obstinacy. At last, when she had squeezed her sickly body between what seemed an endless number of other bodies, she felt the pressure of the crowd suddenly increase as the people pulled back to let the healer and his escort pass through. She felt rather than saw the nearness of the one body she waited for, then with a final effort she reached out quickly between the others and fleetingly seized the rough homespun in her fingers, then let it go and drew back. The stuff had been woven by a woman's hands — dextrous, rapid, women's fingers, pulling, twisting the wool to a fine, even thread, stretching the threads to practiced tautness on the loom, throwing the shuttle with an economical energy that left imagination free to leap and travel. Women's work, taken for granted, expected, despised, yet essential and beautiful.

She let it go, but the feel of the stuff was imprinted on her hand and on her heart, cloth woven by someone who loved him, gritty with dust of much walking, a little warm from its wearer's body. The vitality of that texture of love and work and long wear spread through her weakened body, and she trembled with a violence of reaction to her prolonged struggle, but also with a new sensation, of something pulsing all through her, a strength and liveness almost too great to bear. She swayed, and only the pressure of the crowd kept her upright.

Then all at once the onward movement of the crowd around her slackened and ceased, and she heard the question: "Who touched me?" She heard the bewildered and slightly exasperated response, for what sense did such a question make in the packed crowd, and why the delay, when a child's life was at stake and her father a person of importance? This, after all, was a chance for the young preacher to be accepted in the circles that mattered, among the wealthy and influential. He should not hesitate at such a time. The woman in the shadows shook and gasped painfully, hoping and fearing to hear that voice again. It came again and she could not escape it. "Someone did touch me. I felt the power go out of me," and she knew it had and she knew she could not refuse to respond to that voice. Without giving herself time to reflect she pushed forward once more, but this time with the vigor of a hope that was rapidly becoming certitude. She fell at his feet in the small space created for her by his commanding gesture, and told the whole story, out loud, unashamed. She made public that which had condemned her, which had made her a thing to be pitied but avoided as unclean, a sinner punished by God for sins of her own or her parents or forebears. It was necessary for her to tell the whole humiliating tale of oppression and shame, so that by telling she might claim the healing not only of her body but of the spiritual misery of her rejected years. When the common, dreary tale was told she was not rejected but welcomed, affirmed and acclaimed, her secret shame turned to public blessing.

Among all the stories of healing in the gospels this one is strange and unique, although it has features which evoke themes present and significant in other stories of healing and other encounters of Jesus with women. This woman did not ask aloud for healing, she did not even expect to be consciously noticed. She simply felt that this bodily being, even without awareness, was a bringer of healing. To be in contact with that body, that person, was all she sought, but that she would have at whatever cost, no matter what anyone thought and even though it meant breaking the law which secluded women with her affliction.

In doing this she was one those women who, in the whole experience of what God was doing in Jesus, clung unerringly to the literal truthfulness of incarnation, though they could never have used that word —the sense that God—power, life, growth—was present in this human person.

In the reaching out of her hand she becomes the symbol of all the women who, conditioned and habituated to insignificance, still find in themselves a small flame of unexplainable hope that things may be different, and reach out towards what they recognize in some way as the fire which has lighted their flame. It was in their womanly experience that the women who encountered Jesus found that hope: somewhere in the woman's experience of bodiliness, of process and change and creation as it is known very diversely and physically. The bodies which make them suspect and unclean yet necessary and valued possessions, (the age-old ambivalent valuation of women) were the place of knowledge and of a scarcely communicable wisdom. In the gospel accounts of the encounters of Jesus with women there is this element, this in-touchness, their centering in the physical reality of divine energy in a human wholeness and presence. Incarnation, flesh-taking, being bodily, life itself seen, heard, handled — then and later they did not lose touch with that fact, and when much was inexplicable, that was certain and central.

This made a difference to their sense of religion too, and to their awareness of Jesus as a religious fact. If he was "Messiah" to them, it was in a very different way, one which has continued to be important and is now more important than ever, when the patriarchial and sexist structures of traditional Christianity have become for many women (and men also) a well-nigh impenetrable obstacle to the discovery of Jesus as anything but a tool of oppression.

The masculine mind of Jewish religion thought and dreamed and prayed in terms of conquest, whether by an earthly or a heavenly leader, and many tried to fit Jesus into those dreams, as Christians have done since in so many ways. Whether it be the awesome Christ of Byzantine mosiacs, remote, stern and absolute, or the inspirer of the Crusades, or the image behind such popular hymns as "Onward Christian Soldiers, Marching as to war," the churches have adored a conquering King who crushes the enemy, whether that be pagan hordes or threat of personal sinfulness. And women have seen the Christ similarly, since no other was offered. But not all of them saw him thus — nor all of the men either. Therein lies the possibility of getting in touch with a different Christ, the one who became known to certain women of his own time and later; for these women shared the religion of the people and its dreams and images, since that was the air and food of their nature and culture, but it seems that they did not share them entirely, perhaps because it was clear on reflection that they themselves had no real place in the working out of such dreams and visions. At least their relationship with Jesus was not completely bound up with those dreams, for when he failed to live up to them the women, unlike the men, did not withdraw from him in disillusion, distrust or anger.

Unlike even his closest male followers who clung to him in love but struggled with a rooted inability to make sense of much of what he said, the women seem to have gone straight to the heart of the matter and stayed there. They stayed with Jesus, listening, serving, reflecting together on what they saw and felt, passing on to families, friends and neighbors or strangers the experience they had shared. They stayed until the end and beyond, knowing that in spite of all evidence and all common sense they had to be near that body, living or dead.

This relationship to the bodily reality of Jesus is one of the central facts of the experience of the women, and is part of that re-creation which then began, a re-creation not just of the women, but of the thing which they and Jesus made between them — a new kind of being-together. This was at the heart of the experience of the Kingdom which Jesus proclaimed, yet it has proved impossible for a masculine-dominated culture to live with it, then or since, except in certain strange and unusual situations. These situations have to do with the breakdown (by disaster, or personal or communal disorientation, or by vision or madness) of the normal expectations and customary structures which maintain the stability of a cultural group. But as long as the cultural group remains coherent in its patriarchal basis (benevolent or not) the women are marginal to the more positive aspects of its structures, in terms of opportunity, self-respect, or even the hope of personal satisfaction. Women have little hold on such things and are more easily shaken loose. In the time of Jesus, therefore, their approach to him was less encumbered with preconceptions as well as having that immediacy and wholeness of perception which has come to be called holistic, and which comes more easily to women than to men. It was this uncluttered apprehension of the bodily being of Jesus which lay at the heart of their unquestioning and apparently irrational fidelity, even when the body was dead. The far-reaching results of that deep fidelity need to be further understood, and its significance uncovered for our time.

As for this nameless woman who reached out, we do not know what happened after her healing, but she could have followed either of the two ways into which Jesus often drew the women whose lives he touched.

Perhaps she joined the group of women disciples who travelled with Jesus, and later travelled as missionaries of the new life which was theirs. But perhaps again she stayed in her home town, with results just as far-reaching, for whatever she did she was changed. Released from her diseased condition which had made her "unclean" and forbade any social or sexual intercourse, she could return to the mainstream of daily life, and a woman with the courage to do what she did in search of healing was not one to retire into silence. "Faith" was the quality that the gospel account acclaimed in her, and her faith was made to be shared. Perhaps she became one of the many women who gathered into their homes those who wanted to hear and discuss and pray over the message of new life, sharing with them experiences of healing and hope, guiding and supporting them in their journey of faith, and in time celebrating with them the presence of the risen Lord. The homes of such women became the "household churches" of earliest Christianity.

It is more important than appears at first sight that, as Luke notes, several women around Jesus had been healed of "evil spirits and ailments" (Mary Magdalen, one of the most prominent, had been released from "seven devils," which probably indicates a serious mental illness, and I shall explore the meaning of this in a later chapter). This does not simply mean that they were cured of sickness and were then in good health, as someone might leave the hospital to resume her previous career, for what happened to these women was revolutionary and had results correspondingly disturbing. These women were released not only from the spiritual and physical suffering of whatever disease had afflicted them but from the worse burden of being cut off from life, of feeling useless, unwanted, or positively rejected. The condition of Jewish women was by no means the worst in the history of human societies; indeed the Torah accorded them a dignity and a degree of protection that women in many cultures might have envied. Personal gifts, personal wealth, or the support (or death) of male relatives could allow them prominence in the community and even leadership, yet their status for the most part was little better than that of valuable possessions. Those women who turned to Jesus are not unrepresentative of women in all times who have been and are treated as less than fully human. They were inferior at best, but if there was added to this the burden of sickness (which might often be regarded as the result of their own sin) they could lose the chief claim to value a woman could have, apart from her dowry, which was her ability to serve others and manage her household well, and especially to bear and raise healthy sons. A sick woman was an economic burden and often made to feel it. Though it is true in all times and places that real love can transcend and transform the harshest customs, and personal qualities can triumph over them, it remains true that a legal status of total dependence not only leaves the door wide open to abuse but undermines the very roots of personal self respect. A healthy woman might learn to cope with this and find compensation and satisfaction within the sphere available to her, but a sick woman had little to hope for. To a person in such a state the encounter with the healing power of Jesus meant not merely the removal of an ailment but the experience — perhaps the first experience — of being known and accepted as a person. The woman who suffered from a haemorrhage did not expect such acceptance (one does not hope for the unimaginable) but she and others received it. That experience of unconditional love transformed the whole person, indeed it brought the person into existence, emerging from the twilight life of psychological as well as legal and economic dependence into a fullness of living which rapidly spread into any areas that opened up.

This is the second aspect of the relationship of Jesus with women which leads us into an understanding of the experience he was talking about under the image of "Kingdom". The women were representative of that great assembly of human beings whom Jesus sometimes referred to as "little ones". These were people who in one way or another were regarded by the religious establishment as outcast, or sinners, and included those, for instance, who because of their occupation were ritually unclean, or through pressure of work were unable to keep up the ritual religious requirements. The poor were virtually all in this category. They were "marginal", unconsidered, the "rabble that knows not the law". Women were unclean for a large part of their lives and ritually excluded all their lives, whether in the Temple, where they could not enter the sacred area of sacrifice, or in the Synagogue, where they were purely spectators, behind a curtain or grille. The "little ones" included also those who were outcast not because of economic deprivation but because their livelihood was gained in unacceptable ways, such as prostitution. This group of "tax gatherers and sinners" naturally included many women, whether by their own trade or by association through marriage to a "sinful" man. The sick, of whatever status, were also outcast, not only because sickness generally made them ritually unclean but because it was regarded as probable evidence of being in a state of rejection by God, whether for one's own offenses or those of one's parents. To be a woman was to be less than fully acceptable in any case, though she could gain a kind of secondary acceptability through the support and care she gave to husband and sons. Women, therefore, stood at the very heart of "the poor" to whom Jesus said that he had been called to bring the good news. They knew this, and responded to him with corresponding amazement, gratitude, and whole-hearted commitment. Trying to understand what happened to the women around Jesus is therefore important for understanding the nature of his whole mission, his concept of the "Kingdom" he proclaimed, and the kind of society implicit in that concept. It is even more clearly relevant now, when women's studies of history, and of social and cultural dynamics, have shown more and more clearly how age-old and still flourishing patriarchal societies oppress and distort the lives not only of women but of men, who are equally victims even while they seem to be the "real", the powerful people. The phrase "the feminization of poverty" refers to the fact that the majority of the poor in our culture are women, but it implies that this is new. The fact is, where there has been poverty the women have always been not only the greatest number but the greatest sufferers. A carefully lettered slogan covering a whole side of a home in Belfast proclaims that "the workers are the slaves of capitalism, but women are the slaves of the slaves." As in Belfast (or Lima, or Chicago or London or Tokyo) so in the towns and villages of Galilee and Judea. If Jesus called to the "heavy laden" and laborious, he called most of all to women, the load carriers, the never-resting mothers and wives of the poor. If he proclaimed blessing to the poor, the mourners, the "meek", that blessing and prophecy was one for women.

Trying to uncover the lives and work of women involved in the mission of Jesus and later of the young church requires careful analysis and deduction. It is often a matter of "reading between the lines" in order to discover even the rough indications of the role played by women in the new state of being which Jesus proclaimed. The reason for this is the difficulty his hearers had in dealing with, and later reporting, Jesus' fixed habit of ignoring the usual social and political categories, including those concerned with relations between the sexes. In the political area, for instance, he did not seem to favor those who supported accommodation with the Romans for the sake of stability and prosperity, nor did he side with those who fixed their hopes on the violent overthrow of the occupying power and the establishment of a new Jewish kingdom. People were always trying to align Jesus with one or the other party, but he did not fit the recognized categories, and seemed to demand a manner of human living in which such categories could become irrelevant. Similarly, in his dealings with women he did not seem to suggest reform within the existing categories, demanding for instance greater respect, or stricter regulation of divorce for their protection, though some of his words might be interpreted in such a way. What he was really doing was to refuse to allow the existing political, religious, social or sexual categories to dictate the quality of relationship, whether between debtor and creditor, subject and ruler, servant and master or woman and man. By so doing he actually broke open those categories. Whether he started out with that intention or not, his sense of God, and his encounter with people, drove him to re-discover the meaning of Israel's history of liberation. He ended by rejecting the oppressive structures which still enslaved his people, and positing a new kind of relatedness, social as well as personal, a relatedness symbolized by his table-fellowship with all kinds of people, sharing life as friends.

Jesus took for granted as the basis for his encounters with people a view of human relatedness which transcended any current descriptions, and that made it very hard for those whose minds were formed in the usual categories to give a convincing account of his teaching. There really were no adequate words, and they had to stretch concepts further than they could stand. (This is a permanent difficulty, for no human culture or language can fully express a message that transcends all human divisions, whether conceptual or social). In particular it was hard for men (whether Jew or Gentile) raised in a society that thought of women as more or less desirable adjuncts to the males who were the only full persons, to assimilate such a fundamental alteration in attitudes to the other sex as Jesus was demanding.

It is clear that the New Testament writers were aware of a problem, and Luke in particular stresses incidents in which Jesus gave a new status and importance to women, yet the references are isolated. It is as if Luke had to make a special effort to do justice to this inescapable fact of life in the infant church, yet it was not a natural way for him to think. Paul's ambivalence in this area is notorious. He stresses the irrelevance of all former categories, the radical freedom of the believer from previous laws and customs, and avows openly his personal friendship for and indebtedness to various women whom he claimed as his fellow-workers, which is enough to show how genuine and deep was the change in his own life. On the other hand there was his Jewish background, there was his mindset in a society that took masculine dominance for granted. There was his feeling that in a world soon to end it was desirable to avoid scandal or conflict with unbelievers, and his concern to keep the Christian community orderly and peaceful even at the cost of some sacrifice of principle. (This tendency to sacrifice principle is also illustrated in his willingness to compromise for the sake of peace and order over the matter of love feasts.) For Paul and for those who inherited his teaching all this combined to weigh the balance on the side of custom, at the expense of the new "law of freedom" whenever arguments arose about the role of women.

The whole of the New Testament, then, comes to us through masculine minds of varying degrees of flexibility but all imbued with assumptions which made the male person the norm, though, as we shall see, John's gospel hints at a Christian community that included women quite fully. That is why it can often seem that the attempt to discover the intentions of Jesus towards women work by wrenching the text and inflating quite minor references into points of great significance. In a sense this is true because of the nature of the texts. We explore the significance of chance allusions which for the writer were scarcely significant at all. We pick up hints and string them together to make a pattern. No wonder the process sometimes seems forced.

Yet all this is justified because we begin from a basic Christian assertion — that Jesus proclaimed a new way of human relatedness, one which belongs to the very essence of being human, as God made men and women. Human blindness and fear have created in the world patterns of dominance and subservience, control and submission, possession and dependance, so that the Law is brought in as "holy and just and good", as Paul describes it, since it can at least establish a semblance of justice and respect for human rights against unbridled greed and violence. But Jesus broke through all that and announced a different way. He told women as well as men that they might at last claim the freedom to live in their outward lives, in daily experience, the fact of their deep interrelatedness as creatures, persons whose very being flows out from and back to the inner life of God, and that God known as utter giveness, whose Being is an eternal and unceasing exchange of love among Themselves. That was the message Jesus taught and lived, in his attitudes, his actions, his words, and those who entered into it experienced a bewildering and liberating newness. They struggled to find ways to live that out in their common life as the message spread from city to city and from house to house. They experimented, they fought, they achieved, they failed, they made peace, they tried again, and we can sense that marvelous struggle in the writings which remain to us.

One of the most obvious proofs of the radical shift made by the primitive church in its treatment of normal social distinctions, including sexual ones, is the fact that the rite of baptism was, from the very first, administered to all in exactly the same way. There is no hint that there was ever any doubt about baptizing women (or slaves, or the sick). There are no traces of controversy, or of a different ritual being used for some. Although before long it seemed more fitting that women should be brought to baptism by other women, they were never excluded, and this is a really remarkable fact when we consider how soon distinctions between the sexes began to creep back into other areas of Christian life and observance. We have no record of any words of Jesus, or the earliest church leaders, on the subject, though it seems likely that the words used by Paul emphasizing that "in Christ there is neither Jew nor Gentile, neither bond nor free, neither male nor female" are in fact a quotation from a formula recited during the baptismal liturgy. This absence of precept or comment, combined with universal practice, shows how completely the equal acceptance of men and women in baptism was part of the preaching and living from the beginning. If we compare this with other forms of baptismal rite, such as those of John the Baptist, or of the Qumran community, which were for males only, we can see what a radical break this Christian custom represents. Similarly, women were never excluded from the breaking of bread, although restrictions were soon imposed on their liturgical roles, and they were later excluded from communion during menstruation and after childbirth (picking up once more the Jewish practices). The church has had to live with what were evidently quite basic customs dating back to the ministry of Jesus himself. It is with this startling, radical, shocking and yet for a long time unquestioned inclusion of women in the scope of the good news that we have to reckon in our attempts to understand what Jesus did to human society, challenging it to new experiences of humanness.

We live in a society that has come belatedly and painfully to its awareness of the centuries — indeed the millennia — of oppression of women. In our time it becomes vital to understand better than the earliest church was able to do at the time the essential role of women in that new experience which Jesus offered to all humankind. We need to see what happened to women, and through women to the whole community, and what that means for women now, and through them for the whole community now. From those scant early references we have to draw all that we can, using the best help of biblical scholars and historians. From such work emerges, first of all, a sense of meeting real people, women of vivid and varied character. Through getting to know these women we come to a new awareness of what the message of Jesus was and is. Like the woman who had a haemorrhage, women now are struggling through the indifferent or hostile throng in their efforts to touch the edge of his garment. But, as in her case, the small handful of material we can grasp conveys to us the full power of the person.

Having touched that, we also are summoned to proclaim the healing and hope that have come to us, for this is not a special "women's thing" but the essential message of salvation for the human race. It depends, however, on the women who have the courage to challenge assumptions, ignoring criticism, for the time has passed when women could remain hidden in the crowd, subsumed under the term "man." They are called out to testify publicly what God has done, in the assurance that it is indeed faith which has made them whole persons, never again to disappear into the shadows.

II.
THE WOMAN WITH WATER TO SHARE

One of the tragic results of the age-long oppression of woman in which all the main Christian traditions have been complicit (if not active in promoting it), is that when women brought up in that tradition finally begin to come out of the shadows and recover personhood they find themselves unable to relate to the Christ who is supposed to be the liberator of the oppressed. The relationship prescribed for women towards Christ has been either quite passive, as the female towards the archetypal dominant male, or else quasi-masculine, seeking a degree of freedom to serve by approximating the roles of Christian soldiers and pioneers, thus bypassing, rather than changing, the situation of oppression. This is well demonstrated in the second century Gnostic "Gospel of Thomas" when Peter asks Jesus to expel Mary Magdalen from their company because "women are not worthy of the life." Jesus replies, "See, I shall lead her, so that I will make her male, that she too may become a living spirit resembling you males. For every woman who makes herself male will enter the kingdom." When the choices thus offered are perceived to be equally humiliating and depersonalizing, there is no way to relate to Christ as he has been presented. The fact of his maleness becomes equated with the types of masculine role which have been allotted to him in order to validate a Church structured on masculine models, basically patriarchal, whether monarchical or "democratic." Jesus becomes the symbol of masculine dominance, his maleness used to justify the demand for female subservience, so that for many women who have broken through that conditioning, Jesus is necessarily left behind among the shadows of their abandoned prison.

There is no simple answer to this real experience. It is an important and painful purgation of images and of identity, and its validity has to be affirmed. Yet that cannot be the end of the story, anymore than a phase of transference is the end of the story for a person in the therapeutic process.

The beginning of a re-discovery of what Jesus means for women, and through women, is the realization that it must have been extremely difficult for Jesus to be male in the kind of society into which he was born. The story of the encounter of Jesus with the Samaritan woman shows especially clearly the kind of ease the evangelist allowed him to feel with a woman, as well as her intense surprise and the disapproval of the disciples. His feelings were constrained by the male ethos of his society, and the intimacy of his relationship with Martha and Mary shows the same relaxed feeling we discover by the well. The Samaritan woman, therefore, gives us a way to consider this aspect of the re-creation of Eve, the archetypal woman who was so present to Jesus himself. We need to look first at the psychological background to the aberrant behavior of Jesus as we see it in this encounter.

Men in most societies, and certainly in that of Jesus and in our own, carry the image of the norm. It is their job not only to uphold but to internalize the structures of their society and the values that the structure expresses. In a society which functions by means of competitiveness, rationalism and the suppression of "inappropriate" emotion, the men must be competitive, rational, and able to control their feelings. Those who are not are regarded as, and feel themselves to be, inadequate. In a society which survives by reinforcing its religious identity through strict observance and exclusiveness, which proves its superiority over against others by its level of moral behavior and validates that by pointing to prosperity bestowed on the observant and righteous, the men must be observant, careful of their contacts, sure of their rectitude, and economically secure. Those who are not are a danger to the self-respect of the society, so that they both feel, and are treated as, unacceptable to God and to the other men. But in such societies (and in other varieties such as militaristic ones) it is also inappropriate to show compassion or friendship for the failures and outcasts; to do so is to undermine the values which keep the society stable. Handouts, yes; friendship, no. The lines of demarcation must be kept clear.

In such societies, however, it is permissible for women to have tender feelings, and women have even been encouraged to regard practical compassion for the sick or poor or inadequate as appropriate feminine behaviour. This permission is no threat to the structures, because women are in any case marginal to them, but at the same time it deals conveniently with any moral discomfort which the dominant sex may feel about the plight of inadequate members of society.

Jesus upset all this. From the beginning he expressed strong compassion towards the outcast, indignation at the plight of the poor, and friendship for social menaces of various kinds. He healed the sick, which might well be flying in the face of manifest divine judgement on a sinner; he invited social outcasts to dinner; he spent most of his time with the poor and ignorant and with children. And he really liked these people. He listened to them, talked, told stories, touched them, ate with them, drank with them, joked with them, identified with them. All of this would have been more or less acceptable if done by women. As long as compassion did not get out of hand, a woman would even be encouraged to do at least some of those things in a quiet way. It was the maleness of Jesus that made him a problem and a threat, for he was clearly not himself poor, sick, ignorant or sinful. After a time suggestions that he was indeed sinful, possessed, or at least uneducated did arise, because it was urgently necessary to suggest reasons why a man who had, on the face of it, all the qualifications for a leadership acceptable and even welcome to the establishment was thus betraying his class and his nation, as the nation was defined by those who claimed to guide and represent it.

Jesus as a Jewish male was a scandal, sometimes even to those who loved him and followed him. To his followers his outbursts of anger and grief at the plight of the poor were liberating (because many of them came from among the despised) but also baffling, because instead of inviting them to move up into respectability he seemed to be throwing away their and his own chances of achieving leadership and real power.

It is no wonder that Jesus seems to have found the company and friendship of women a comfort and a relief. They were not the only ones who accepted him, for he was always accepted by the "little ones", but it was possible for women who met him to accept his liberating friendship without strings, since they did not expect to be part of the power structure. They saw and experienced his compassion and were not scandalized. They felt his grief and anger and knew in it a tremendous freedom, because it allowed them to acknowledge their own grief, and their own anger at the suffering around them and in their lives. He gave them permission to share that compassion and grief and anger, and to know that in feeling these things they were acceptable to a God who, according to Jesus, felt exactly the same way.

John's gospel presents the story of a woman who stumbled unexpectedly on the experience of acceptability and found it both unnerving and liberating. It is an interesting story, no doubt reflecting the presence in the Johannine church of the theological debate involving women as well as men, and clear evidence of the role of women as preachers, apostles, and above all, disciples, which is John's most important category. In John's gospel a man and a woman stand together beneath the cross, the first witness and preacher of resurrection is a woman, and the Samaritan woman, like Nicodemus, receives a deep revelation. The stories of Nicodemus and of the Samaritan woman are parallels. There is in both the same kind of encounter, and Jesus is shown preaching to both with challenge as well as sympathy, but there is contrast too, for this equal treatment is given to two people who represent the opposite ends of the spectrum of social and religious acceptability in Jewish society. One is male, a leader in Israel, learned, upright and respected; the other is female, marginal even in her own village, ignorant, morally suspect, and belonging to a people who are religiously heretical in Jewish eyes. That Jesus should be presented as revealing deep and startling insights to a man like Nicodemus is what any observer of Jesus, seeing him in the setting and expectations of his religion, would want and applaud. That he would treat the woman of a despised people in exactly the same way is not a mark of what some spiritual writers have offensively called his "condescension", but of his way of being, on occasion, quite oblivious to the normal taboos which keep any society orderly and predictable.

It was this habit of walking right through social and religious barriers that the contemporaries of Jesus found so hard to deal with. They operated out of expectations which they assumed he shared, but often found his words and behaviour not so much opposing them as simply ignoring them. He seemed to work on a set of assumptions of his own, which he sometimes attributed to his Father, but often didn't bother to explain at all.

His attitude to women seems to have been one of those areas where he made no explanation, or if he did his hearers found the explanation too odd or shocking, for it has not survived. His attitude also left his followers in a difficult position, for it was clear that he expected those who came with him to share his approach. It was a basic fact of his behaviour and they had to make what they could of that. In the story of the Samaritan woman we have a vivid instance of this, both in the way the encounter itself is presented, and in the account of the disciples' reaction to it. It is a deeply important introduction to our understanding of Jesus with women because unless we postulate that this is a fictional episode, a theological discussion given a provocative setting for didactic purposes, we have to recognize that the story must have come to the evangelist from one of the two principals, Jesus himself, or the woman, whether directly or indirectly.

I am among those who incline to the belief that basic elements of the Gospel of John were composed by John-bar-Zebedee, probably over a number of years and through several stages of development and commentary in response to the growth of a young church, though it was possibly edited and finally put together after his death. This view of the authorship and early dating is regaining respectability among Scripture scholars, after a period of more or less compulsory late dating, and while it does not alter our assessment of the theological depth and motivation of John's gospel, it does change our estimate of how much light this gospel throws on the thought and behaviour of Jesus himself as his friends knew him. If, as many now believe, much of the material in the fourth gospel was written by a close friend, and contains some of the earliest of all gospel material (as well as much later reflection and theological development) then we have something of startling interest: the impression made on a sensitive, reflective and creative mind by daily contact with Jesus over a period of many months, perhaps years. It is not reporting (though a few incidents do have the racy, immediate quality of an imaginative eyewitness report) but it is vivid evocation drawing on actual memory, and memory in this context means the retentive, well-practised memory of a society in which most religious teachings (of disciples by the Rabbis, or of children in Synagogue schools) was oral.

We have the conversation with the Samaritan woman at third hand.

We can assume that Jesus told his disciples about it, perhaps not all at once but in various conversations when similar themes were being developed. And John made use of what he remembered of those conversations, putting them together in a coherent account for his purposes. (This is true of several such dialogues in John's gospel, and I shall be drawing on others in the course of this book). But the memories on which the account drew (and this is true even if we prefer a late dating) may include not only whatever Jesus mentioned of his encounter, but the impression made on the disciples themselves by the aftermath, when they stayed in the Samaritan village at Jesus' insistence, and perhaps heard the woman herself and her neighbors. Or the woman, or others who knew her and her story, may have formed part of the Johannine church later on, and brought their story with them.

Someone once wrote a book called *How Many Children Had Lady Macbeth?*, a question which is irrelevant to Shakespeare's intention, and illegitimate to literary criticism, yet if Lady Macbeth was an historical character — as indeed she was — we might legitimately seek answers to questions which were quite beside the point for Shakespeare. So with the scriptural authors. If we are to understand their minds, and the people they evoke for us, we need to look at the experiences which influenced them, yet which they never mention, to build up a picture which properly includes things that were irrelevant to their purposes as writers.

It is by such a use of imagination drawing on available data that we can become aware of the significance of an occasion when Jesus felt very much in touch with another human being. It was near the beginning of that stage of his life which followed the shattering experience of the baptism in the Jordan and its aftermath in the wilderness, when the foundation of reality had split open and he had felt in himself a demand so deep, insistent and dangerous that it required the rediscovery of every aspect of his world. The subsequent time was a slow, jerky and painful process of testing, experiment, reaching out. In his search for the meaning of himself and his mission he was constantly confronting the stereotypes, the fixed images and expectations, with which others tried to clothe their experience of him and make him safe and manageable. He was attracting others, touching minds, feeling their response, sharing, changing; yet in them too the experience was uneven, blocked, often perverse. It was exciting but it was also exhausting.

He was tired in spirit and his physical fatigue reflected that. He sent his followers on ahead to buy supplies, needing rest but needing solitude also — time to reflect, uninterrupted, on the relationships that were developing. Among his new followers he felt alone because of the weight of strange knowledge as yet unclear. There was much he could not explain. And there was in him a power and fear and a need to relate the new, overwhelming messages of personal experience to the old and mighty messages of his peoples' history and hopes. He needed solitude because he was alone.

Into that needful solitude someone intruded, a woman coming along to fetch water at an inappropriate time of day, in the heat of midday rather than with the other women in the cool of the morning or evening. Here was another person isolated as he felt isolated. He could have ignored her, and she would have fetched her water and gone, as indeed she expected to do, since he was a Jew and Jews did not talk with Samaritans, nor respectable men with chance-met women. But he reached out to her, made contact with out excuse or explanation. He established contact by asking for something which she was able to give, a very simple request from one person to another. It was good to be able to do that, and there was something in the woman's attitude and personality which made it possible. Her first response of surprise, even a little mockery, is that of one who is not conditioned to subservience. Perhaps because of her less than respectable relationships with men she was free of some of the usual feminine constraints. She had an easiness and openness about her which made it possible for her to meet this stranger with comradely curiosity, as one unconventional person to another. It seems in keeping with the topsy-turvy quality of God's Kingdom that the "bad" woman is more open, human and interested in people than a "good" one might have been.

Perhaps it was this that made him able to share so much with her. Strange convictions were stirring in him, an awareness of what he had to give, if only someone were willing to ask for it, as he had asked for water. Only the need could evoke the response. His ideas spilled over, striving to be received, and the woman, fascinated and touched, yet uncertain in this strange experience, tried to pin it down to familiar things. If he spoke of water then so did she, as she understood that, yet well aware of the unnerving implications of what she was saying. "Are you greater than our ancestor, Jacob?" It was only partly an ironic question and his reply took it seriously, yet went beyond it. She had to keep to the tone of slight mockery. It was part of her usual defense, her protection of the sensitive person others must not see, and it was something to hold on to in this strange experience, but her response was deep. And Jesus' request to her to fetch her husband was an indication that he knew, and she knew, the importance of this encounter. He showed her, then, that his willingness to share so deeply with her was not dependent on any false estimate of her. John's brief account condenses what must have been a longer sharing, which opened up to her much she had thought secret. It brought healing to many sore experiences. He took her as she was, without condemnation or comment, and the realization of this broke down her defenses. He accepted her, shared things that were evidently of deep importance to him; he had shown need, not just for water but need for her response. He didn't care about the things that should have put a strong barrier between them. How, then, would such a man deal with the deep divisions of religion?

As it was to most women, the male power-struggle ("on which mountain?") was meaningless to her but it was a fact of her life, one that had to be reckoned with. Perhaps if that were settled one could concentrate on essentials. The response she got was not of the kind she expected, in favor of one side or the other, which was and is how the argument is always set out. He simply rejected that ground of debate altogether. He moved her into an area she, as a woman, knew well: the ground where life begins.

The response is one we need. The real worship, the living water of self-giving in love, is as irrepressible as a mountain spring. In some places the springs are known, the ways to them well trodden, with, alas, the danger that anxious people may try to fence them off from thirsty undesirables. Or hidden water may spring up, bringing life richly and quietly, but unnoticed. But the outpouring of life is one — it wells up from one deep source.

It welled up in the mind of the woman and fumblingly she tried to express her sense of standing somehow at the heart of a mystery, but needing, for confirmation of her awareness, the voice that could authentically speak out of that mystery. "When he comes he will tell us everything." Everything? The word seems to reflect a genuinely remembered turn of phrase, an ebullient feminine habit of using exaggeration as a way of conveying fullness. Later she would say, "He told me *everything* I ever did," and the obviously inaccurate phrase would reflect her sense of the wholeness with which he embraced her shabby and suffering life. The one who will tell "everything" is not one who will talk and talk, announce detailed apocalyptic prophecies, but one who opens the way into all reality, releasing the hidden spring which is in each one, yet common to all. And he responded by confirming her scarcely articulated awareness.

There is something almost comic about the interruption, the breaking off of a communication so simple and whole just at that point. The disciples returned and suddenly the deep truthfulness of need, hope and discovery between two human beings was reduced to a complicated social awkwardness. The disciples felt a need to excuse an encounter that should not have happened. Evidently they felt they were relieving Jesus of an embarrassment, for the woman left immediately. Why he had not got rid of her before they could not understand and didn't quite like to ask. Even their as yet small experience of him made them feel it would be wiser and more comfortable not to know the reason.

She left her water jar behind, a detail John mentions thoughtfully. She no longer needed it, in a sense, for she carried within her the spring of water he had promised, and she knew it. And a spring is not private. It is the birth of a river from which many will drink and wash, on which much traffic will pass.

The people in the village knew the woman; she had her essential place, she was part of the pattern. The outcast and despised, the dark side of a community's life, are as necessary to the social design as the light. The villagers knew her as a humorous, erratic, skeptical, independent person who would fight and survive — certainly not the righteous type. What they saw in her that day was a change so startling that it moved several, at least, out of the pattern which she no longer fitted.

The offer of living water was, it seemed, accepted by some people in that place, outcast heretics though they were. John's church probably had contact with a church that later grew there. Something happened, a group of people gathered themselves around a proclamation of good news. What did those Samaritans hear and believe? If the news was good for them it was because the doom which Jesus (and John the Baptist before him) clearly announced was, it seemed, avoidable through the response of the "little ones". Somehow the God he was in touch with could draw hope out of the heart of alienation, when all categories were smashed.

It was not long, even among the earliest Christian communities, (at least in those originating from Jerusalem, and from Paul), before the message was domesticated and modified, because people could not live with the starkness of that absence of social categorizing. Samaritans and women might indeed be members of the new Way, but the awful simplicity of Jesus was too much to live with; there had to be barriers, codes, expectations and patterns of social behaviour. How else could community life develop? The doom of Jerusalem, and of the Jewish nation, came. Jesus had known it would unless something greater came first, but the lesson was not learned. Jesus' alternative to doom, the clarity of the new creation, could not take root. Something new did break through, but could not altogether translate the old, or supersede it. It could only give it, perhaps, another chance, more time, before the final doom.

The history of Christianity is the story of how that time was used. On the whole it was used to try to make Jesus' vision fit into some given patten of social and philosophical expectation which the people concerned regarded as "normal". And "normal" has meant, until recently, "right" and "permanent", because the sense of the scale of history is quite a recent experience, and it was easily possible to feel that the system one had grown up in (which therefore conditioned all one's expectations) was the "real" one, though undoubtedly other imperfect or barbaric systems had previously prevailed, until they were superseded by the "right" one. The attitude of, for instance, the eighteenth century intelligentsia to the customs of the middle ages was not that the middle ages were *different* but that they were *wrong*: "gothic" — that is, repulsively barbaric. Their "present time" was not perfect but that was only because not all human beings were yet prepared to accept the *right* way of thinking and acting. But in its time the society of medieval Europe (enormously varied as it was) had also regarded itself as patterned on a divine model, which could be perfected, since the Church contained in itself the reflection of the heavenly hierarchy. All other societies were heathen or heretic, outside and outcast. The categories recognized by the Church (quite unaware of its own cultural conditioning) or the later categories of "polite" society in the Enlightenment *were* the shape of reality, to the people who lived by them. For them, change could only mean either progress towards a more perfect realization of this given model, or some attack on, and breakdown of, that model caused by enemies within or without.

Yet, throughout the depressing history of attempts to process Christianity according to some "normal" social and philosophical model, there have been moments — hundreds, thousands of them — when the thing Jesus did happened again, when categories were broken in the name of the gospel, people encountered each other through the gaps, the water of life flowed freely, strange new plants began to grow, and the world changed. The experience was so powerful and so heady that it often scared not only the authorities, as in the time of Jesus, but also the people it happened to, and they themselves tried to contain it, to give it a manageable shape, an explanation. We can think, for instance, of the impulse to freedom in a woman like Teresa of Avila, convinced that the love she had come to know really could be lived among a group of women who believed in it. In order to make that possible it was necessary to reject many of the existing patterns of status and religion, and opt for something so basic in terms of life-style that it couldn't be used to categorize. On the other hand, for its survival, it had to be physically enclosed, separated from those who would categorize and control. So the means to freedom became also, very easily, the creation of another category, as restrictive as the old.

Many medieval sects, and later the Quakers and new world Utopians like the Oneida community, smashed categories as they were seized with the sense of the freedom to encounter and love which the Gospel proclaimed. They discarded private possessions and held things in common, even, in some cases, their sexuality. They sought ways to embody their vision, and they terrified "normal" people, whose security was threatened as the male disciples' security was threatened by Jesus' behaviour towards women. Yet, if they survived the mob, the heresy hunters, or the law, they also were subject to the tendency to create new restrictions to replace the old, categorizing and separating, unable to trust the experience which had inspired them.

There seemed to be no other way to survive. Perhaps there wasn't, since imagination could not stretch to a real alternative. Yet if we read the gospel accounts of the behaviour of Jesus towards outcast people, and especially women, we cannot escape the awareness that, for him, the water of life which sprang in each person was between them, and was the divine life which was his life, and simply did not take account of categories and customs. Of its nature it could not do so, and to erect any protective barrier was to limit the power of life itself.

It was not a blind force, nor was the person in whom the water sprang up to eternal life merely a passive receptacle. Rather, the person herself *was* the water, the life, and she must act in accordance with the nature of that life. That was what the Samaritan woman began to do, and no doubt continued to do, for the account of what happened between her and the others in her village can only have come at some stage from surviving memories within the little church which developed in that place and from that encounter. When, later on, Peter and John were summoned to believers in Samaria (Acts 8:14) they were not visiting a group of completely new converts. (If they had been converted by a member of the Jerusalem church the experience of the Spirit "coming on them" would not have been unfamiliar to them, as it evidently was.) Peter and John more probably went to a group which had developed in belief and hope but in isolation; hearing of the great out-pouring of life following Pentecost, they hoped to understand their own gift better through these other followers of the Christ who had once visited them. Perhaps at the heart of that gathering was the woman who began it all. The internal evidence of John's gospel indicates that there were Samaritan elements in the Johannine church, and perhaps the memory of this pioneer was precious to them.

She was not the only woman around whom a church developed, a gathering of searching and hoping people. The divine power released through such outcasts, called from the margins into the heart of life, was immeasurable, truly an inner spring always welling up to eternal life. But it is only now that we can begin to appreciate the scope of such an outpouring. Because we need no longer be caught in the illusion of one inevitable and "right" system, because we have an awareness of the terrifying and yet invigorating nature of social and religious reality as a great river rather than a still pool, because we can understand at least a little (whether through Jungian symbols or through the new physics) of the mind-boggling intricacy of interrelatedness in ourselves and in all creation: because of all this we can grasp, as never before, the significance of what Jesus was really doing when he talked to the woman at the well and what John, and his readers, were experiencing when they shared that story. Jesus was not setting out to shock (though he did sometimes find it appropriate to do that). He was simply reaching out in need to another human being who responded out of her complex and (until then) half-conscious and unadmitted need. And the meeting was powerful, and released a flood which washed away, unnoticed, huge and apparently immovable social and religious barriers.

Hard as it has tried, official Christianity has never been able to rebuild the barriers as strongly as that. Firm and well-defended as they have been through the centuries, there has always been the subversive force within, the gospel itself interacting with the human heart longing for freedom, a power strong enough to undermine and sweep away the re-erected barriers. (No wonder it seemed safer, for many generations, to announce the gospel in a language only the establishment could understand. And even that didn't work.)

At this time we are without excuse if we continue to build barriers, for we cannot plead the historical and cultural myopia of our ancestors. If we do not see it is because we will not, but say we do. "Because you say 'we see' your guilt remains," John has Jesus say. We need to take seriously the command of Jesus to smash the barriers, simply as a matter of survival, for the barriers we have built are imprisoning us. They are keeping us passive while the powers of darkness (by definition, therefore, blind powers) prepare to destroy life, whether by nuclear war, or (more slowly) by pollution of soil, water and air until they become incapable of sustaining healthy life anymore, or to control and condition life to become a usable asset for those in power.

The smashing of barriers which Jesus initiated is the only strategy for survival, because it allows people to touch and know each other without fear, and therefore to act together for their own good and the good of others. And the women are more easily the initiators of this strategy, because the feminine type of consciousness is one which emerges from within and judges by quality of feeling rather than by exterior categories, unless the women have been conditioned to do otherwise, at least superficially. It is a human consciousness we all need, men and women, but women especially are aware of it and are claiming the needfulness of it. It is Jesus' strategy, speaking to the depth in people, being heard at that point where they are most themselves but also most in touch with others. It calls them together, to live a different kind of relationship, one which is not constituted by inherited or imposed categories, devised for the safety and dominance of one group or other, but only by the sharing of the waters of life.

What that means in practice is ours to discover, but the practical consequences, their problems and their opportunities, are already to be discerned in the experience of the women of the New Testament and other little ones as they tried to live out the results of their encounters with Jesus. Then and now, women disciples have to deal not only with male hostility but with male embarrassment, the floundering awkwardness of people plunged into this deep water when old categories have let them down. Women also have to deal more urgently still with their own uncertainties and fears, their own scarcely admitted hankering after the safety and predictability of a position of subjection and dependence, however well disguised. Our situation is very different, yet in the encounter of women with Jesus we see the roots of our own fears and hopes, and the vision of how living water might be released into a thirsty world.

III.
"THE BEST PART"

There is only one figure in the New Testament of whom it is said that wherever the good news is proclaimed that person's deed of love will be proclaimed in it. The action so signalized by the evangelist as worthy of praise was not a miracle of healing, or a powerful preaching, or even martyrdom. It was a piece of rather eccentric and socially embarrassing behaviour, an action which would understandably be criticized as wasteful and stupid, or as an hysterical display of unseemly emotion. Yet the story of the women who anointed Jesus has indeed been told "whereever the gospel is preached"; it has been lovingly evoked in pictures and poems, and gratefully dwelt on in prayer.

Who was this woman, and why did she do what she did? John says she was Mary, Martha's sister, and indeed the roles of the two sisters at this dinner party are perfectly in character. Of course Martha would be "serving", which would mean she was in charge of the whole organization of a big social occasion, for she was the head of what was clearly a well-to-do household, perhaps as a widow. And of course Mary would be doing something unexpected and rather outrageous, and of course Jesus would be supporting and even encouraging her! But Matthew and Mark don't name the woman, and Luke tells a story of an unnamed "sinful" woman who anointed the feet of Jesus when he was a dinner guest in a wealthy home in Galilee, in the early part of his ministry. Because of this some have surmised that Mary of Bethany had once been a "sinner" and had been converted by Jesus in Galilee, and in Bethany was recalling that earlier encounter. One strong tradition has identified the sinful woman with Mary of Magdala, and has even tried to identify her with Martha's sister also, because there seems to be the same kind of impulsive and passionate devotion in all three characters. Some scholars have simply assumed that the story went through several different versions before it was written by different evangelists, or that incidents from different events became confused. Any of these is possible, and there is no way we can find a perfectly tidy explanation for the differences.

It is not even clear what the woman actually did, for Matthew and Mark have her anointing the head of Jesus, which would be a relatively normal gesture, though extravagant, but John has her anointing his feet, and in Luke's account she weeps over them and in both she wipes them with her hair. No amount of ingenuity can make a plain tale out of all this, yet the story has been so precious to people of faith that these details have never worried them, and that is because the insight of faith somehow touches a deeper kind of consistency in the stories. It is this kind of approach, seeking to be in touch with the feelings of those involved, which can help us to understand better the actual human beings from whose experiences the various accounts are woven. For the importance of the story is clear from the beginning; all four evangelists tell it in one form or another and three of them place it as a kind of "gateway" to the story of the passion of Jesus, a symbolic prologue to the last act of the drama of salvation.

It is therefore important for us to enter imaginatively into the experience which made such an incident possible. We need to understand it not only by studying the text to discern the authors' methods and intentions but by getting behind them to the people and circumstances. What kind of woman was this? Why did she do this? Why has it seemed so important?

One of the facts we have to keep remembering is that the women around Jesus formed a group, even though we may meet them individually in certain incidents. They did not, like actors, appear suddenly on the stage, give their brief performance and then disappear. They were real people, they had a human context, belonging to the group of the disciples of Jesus, those who had chosen to follow him and learn from him, and who later became the nucleus of men and women called to proclaim the kingdom of God. The group included the Twelve but there were many more, and a number of them were women. We know the names of only a few, but Luke says they were numerous. Some of these were women who had left their homes and travelled the country with Jesus. Some were wives of disciples, perhaps some were widows, some seem to have been simply women of independent spirit, brave enough to break with custom as Jesus did and withstand the hostility and vilification which would normally result. In any case they were doing something very strange in leaving their domestic role, and we can see here more clearly than anywhere else how Jesus' explicit calling of women as disciples, and his whole treatment of them, was a direct challenge to the placing of women in a position of subjection, as possessions of their fathers or husbands.

Of the women who travelled with Jesus the phrase used is "they followed him", a phrase which itself indicates that they were disciples and "followed" the Lord as did Simon, James and the rest. It seems these women helped to handle the practical arrangements for the group (quite a challenge to catering skills, under the circumstances) but there were also those who provided hospitality for the disciples in their own homes as Martha and Mary did, and Peter's family. Although the synoptics do not mention this, if we can take the Samaritan woman as an indication some women disciples also preached, as did the men. But there was no special division according to function; they all knew each other. These women were drawn together by their love for the Master, but also by the fact that, as women, they were not fully accepted as disciples by the men, for no matter what Jesus might do or say his male followers could not quite overcome the ingrained cultural attitudes to females. So the women depended a great deal on each other, and they encouraged and supported each other in their discipleship, especially by telling and retelling to each other the stories of their own healings, their own coming to discipleship. They cherished any stories of encounters of Jesus with women, many of which they themselves, or at least some among them, had witnessed.

We have a very clear account from Luke (10:38-42) of one occasion on which Jesus expressly indicated and upheld the full discipleship of women. The fact that Luke found this incident remembered and recorded among the material he collected, and felt it important to include it in his gospel, is itself an indication both that the discipleship of women was a point of difficulty for the early communities (it needed to be defended and spelled out) and that such discipleship was known to be part of Jesus' plan for the Kingdom. In a sense, Luke plays down the active discipleship of women; they are easily categorized in the catering area, or as sick persons in need of healing, which in a way makes it all the more interesting that he indicates this strong bit of evidence.

The famous little story of Martha and Mary has been interpreted by later spirituality as a vindication of the "useless" contemplative over against the "useful" activist and that is perhaps a legitimate application, but it is a later extension of the meaning of an incident which is essentially about something quite different. For what Mary was doing was "sitting at the feet" of Jesus, which was a technical phrase referring to the stance of the accredited disciple toward a Master, as Saul "sat at the feet" of the great Rabbi Gamaliel. Mary, a woman, was sitting there among the men. She had adopted the stance and role of a disciple, which was a thing expressly forbidden to women, and Martha's intervention was not so much the grievance of an over-worked housewife as a shocked reaction to a breach of expected feminine behaviour. Martha's reaction perhaps shows us also how hard it was to grasp the whole scope of the liberation brought by Jesus, for Martha herself believed, and loved and was loved by Jesus, and was a leader in her own right. Mary's behaviour meant that Martha had more to do, naturally, and her complaint was based on the expectation in all societies of a division of labor between sexes, but it is an expectation which has always tended to harden into a moral and religious principle, rather than a matter of convenience.

So Jesus was being asked to uphold what seemed not only the law of his religion but the demand of natural justice, and indeed the sympathies of many have gone out to harassed and exasperated Martha. The response of Jesus was first of all a complete vindication of Mary's right to stay where she was, not only on this occasion but permanently, but it annexed something else of equal importance: "The part that Mary has *chosen* is best." He affirmed her right and power to choose a thing of which women were socially and religiously deprived. She, like the men, had made a free choice, and that should not be taken from her. Moreover, what she and they had chosen was "the best"; that is the foundation of everything else. Whatever else they did must be done in the context of that choice of discipleship. That is "the one thing necessary". If they chose, as many of the women around Jesus apparently did, also to be concerned with cooking and catering and hospitality generally, they did so *as disciples*, freely choosing their own practical way of exercising discipleship, but not being thereby debarred from listening to Jesus, or themselves teaching, healing and calling others.

That was the message, the experience, which the group of women around Jesus shared, and talked about together. There were many stories of how that freedom to choose had been experienced, and expressed, and perhaps among these stories was the strange tale of a woman who, in the urgency of her need to be with Jesus, had broken in on a dinner party in a wealthy home.

It happened in Galilee, in the early days, and it had naturally been much talked of. The host had been a prominent person, a Pharisee, who had graciously invited the popular new preacher to his house. Perhaps he did it out of curiosity, perhaps with a real desire to understand better, perhaps with the kindly intention of introducing the young man to learned and influential people who would direct and correct his wayward but impressive gifts as a teacher. But the outcome was not as intended, and what stayed in the minds of the guests, and of all those who heard about it from them or from the servants, was the disruption of the party by a woman from the town. She was a well-known woman of bad character, quite unacceptable in any God-fearing household, and her behaviour there had caused reactions of shock, disgust, and also laughter and cynical nods and winks, for this female had poured expensive ointment over the feet of Jesus and cried over them as well in the most maudlin fashion, and then used her *hair* (would you believe it?) to wipe them with. But the most shocking thing had been the attitude of Jesus himself, for instead of withdrawing from her polluting touch, or reproving her and telling her to change her life, he had appeared to welcome her caresses. He even defended her in a way that compared her favorably with his host. Clearly, there was something between them, the gossips said shrewdly. Maybe this Teacher was not so holy after all.

But some heard the story and drew different conclusions. Perhaps the women who told each other the story had known her. Perhaps she became one of them. Was she after all the same woman called Mary who came to him at Bethany? We cannot tell, but we can feel a link, and perceive why tradition wanted to identify the two, for in the minds of all the women this story must have been a source of consolation and a subject for their conversations and reflections, since they also had been changed and healed by the touch of a love beyond anything they had ever experienced or imagined. They too had been enabled to *choose*, to become other, to be disciples. They knew how that woman felt, they knew how Jesus responded. They pondered together the meaning of the story, they discussed the details of it — the anointing, the weeping, the acceptance, the affirmation of freedom to choose and change.

All this had happened as much as two years before the dinner party at Bethany, and much had taken place since. Those early days of huge popularity and hopefulness were passed, there was a mounting tide of hostility among the religious leaders of the people, and because of that a fear and unease among those who depended on the approval of these leaders for their religious status and respectability, which meant often their chances of employment. The mass of the people were still with Jesus and ready to follow if he seemed to be leading them towards freedom from religious and secular oppression, yet they were puzzled and disillusioned by the things he said, confused by criticism, easily persuaded. He had withdrawn from Jerusalem to remote places; he was not attracting the support either of the resistance movement of the Zealots, or of the official leaders, and it was hard to see how a Messiah could succeed without one or the other of those groups to back him. On the contrary, he seemed to be antagonizing people, even those who had followed him, by his gloomy prophecies, his condemnations of official hypocrisy, his constant refusal to choose the methods necessary for a popular leader. Was he a friend of Rome, some were asking, or maybe just another deluded pseudo-Messiah?

More and more people were doubtful or critical or worried, and the talk among the disciples themselves was uneasy. Families were suggesting they should reconsider their commitment to a man who seemed headed into serious trouble. (We can tell from the gospel warnings how large the subject of family influence and conflict loomed in the minds of the early followers.) They didn't agree among themselves about the meaning of the things Jesus was telling them. When they were with him they trusted him completely, but when they listened to people in the streets, or to the worries of their families, or heard the denunciations by the leaders of the synagogues or the Pharisees, they wavered, and felt sick with unnamed doubts. The words of Jesus himself were not reassuring, with their images of coming disaster, of persecution and death. Of course, they said to each other, he must be feeling the pressure himself, he's depressed and prey to morbid fancies, not himself — but however often they told each other that all would be well there was unspoken fear and tension. Groundless quarrels flared up, they watched each other distrustfully yet clung together for comfort.

The women watched, and listened. They knew the gossip better than any, for it was they who fetched water and brought food for the group. They talked with other women at the wells and in the markets, they knew the feeling among the people. But they also listened to Jesus, and they heard him in a different way. As people who knew what it meant to be powerless, they had no investment in dreams of conquest, which would leave them exactly where they were before. Also, because of what he had done for them, and just because they were women, they were sensitive to him in a special way — to his feelings, and his unspoken messages. They saw how he was hurt by the rejection he increasingly encountered, and even more deeply hurt by the incomprehension of his friends. They listened, they heard and they pondered, putting together in their intimate conversations his own words about suffering to come. and the words of the prophets he so often quoted. They, as much as the men, were worried, and at a loss to understand the contradictions between the expectation of a Messiah and the path he seemed to be taking, yet they knew there must be a meaning in it all. Their trust in him was too deep to be altered, for it rested on an awareness of him as a person, which had become part of their own self-awareness as persons. He seemed so much to need and want some kind of understanding, some affirmation in the loneliness of his choice, yet they could not speak out what they felt, it was too confused, impossible to express. Even though they were his disciples most of them may have been more hesitant than the men to approach him directly. Their freedom as disciples was a fact they had to learn to live with and use, it grew gradually; they could not easily be free of the conditioning that had kept them so long subservient and silent. Yet as the days passed, and the weeks, they longed more and more to let him know that some at least of his friends believed in whatever choices he was making, were with him in his struggle, and would not be alienated by anything he might do or say.

Perhaps it was during this time that one of them recalled and retold the story of the woman in Simon's house, and gave it a new resonance. Many people had been shocked by that event, but to these women it was precious, for it told of a woman who had found a way without words to show her sorrow and her love. Anointing was for the kings of old, wasn't it? And for the priests, and as a gesture of honor for a guest, but it was also for the dead, to prepare for burial. They believed he was Messiah, the Christ, and the very word meant "anointed". If their Christ were indeed doomed to die, even that must somehow have meaning, as the prophecies seemed to hint. They could not make sense of it, but even in that he must know their devotion and trust. In some such way the thought grew, and there was one among the women who said to the others, "Let us do as she did — let us show him our understanding and love". That one gave imaginative direction to the feeling of the group, for she was the kind of person who takes initiatives and sees visions. Perhaps she was Mary of Bethany, who had watched her brother die, and had seen the power of life overcome death in him. She, more than the others perhaps, knew obscurely that death might not be the all-powerful enemy.

Perhaps it was the knowledge that a great dinner was to be given which brought reflection to the point of action, just such a dinner as the one in Galilee. It was in the house of "Simon the Leper". Was he a leper who had been healed? Or, since he is not mentioned as being at the dinner, was he perhaps the deceased father of Martha and Mary and Lazarus? Was the name a coincidence or a confusion? In any case Martha and Mary and other women were serving, for it was a big party, evidently including many of Jesus' male disciples as well as neighbors and friends. This large gathering, this "banquet given in his honor," was probably a deliberate public gesture of support for Jesus by people who were well-to-do and locally important, at a time when many were turning against him. If so it was the right time for the women to reinforce that affirmation by a symbolic ritual gesture of great power. Even the idea for the banquet possibly came from Martha and Mary themselves.

In the years that followed, the action of the women in the house of Simon the Leper was told and retold by different people and in different places. Many people, both friends and enemies, heard that while the dinner was in progress, a woman came in and anointed Jesus with expensive perfume. It was a royal anointing, on his head, so said one version of the tale. And some of the disciples had objected, it was said, on the grounds of wasteful expense, and Jesus had defended her; it was for his burial, he had said, and in retrospect the tellers of the tale acknowledged the rightness of the gesture.

Many years later John Mark wrote his gospel in Rome, for gentile

Christians, drawing on such accounts of an event he had not witnessed, though possibly he was nearby, as a young boy, at the time. The writer of Matthew wrote from the same collection of memories and stories and Luke picked a tale of an earlier anointing, or the same one told differently by different people, and his witnesses placed it in Galilee, so presumably he ignored any other settings as merely repetition. But John's gospel, as so often, gives us vivid details which are the mark of an eyewitness. John's eye for detail enables us to enter the scene and understand the universal human feelings, for he (or at least his informant, if the evangelist was not John) was present at that dinner.

John tells us that it was Mary who brought in a large flask of ointment. I have supposed that she was there of behalf of the other women, but she was there also for all those who since that time have longed to show their love and to share in the dedication of Jesus. The ointment was very expensive; perhaps they pooled their resources to buy it, or perhaps it had been part of someone's dowry, kept safely and never used.

It was probably towards the end of the meal, when people were relaxed and conversing over their wine, that Mary came in, unnoticed at first among the women who moved quietly in and out with more wine, or sweetmeats. As she came, the other women paused and gathered quietly near the doorway. She came to him as he reclined at table, and suddenly there was a little sharp snap as the seal of the alabaster phial broke, and in a moment the scent of it filled the whole house. As the glory of God filled the House when God summoned Isaiah to prophecy, as the Cloud of the presence filled the House at its dedication, so now the symbol of a greater prophecy and a more profound dedication anointed the Temple of his body and filled the house with its sweetness. It struck the senses of all, and a silence fell on the room as the guests realized what was happening. Some knew the story of the earlier anointing, all knew Mary, and the deep and tender relationship between Jesus and Mary and her sister and brother. And there indeed sat Lazarus at the side of Jesus, living symbol of a power stronger than the fear of death which hovered at the backs of many minds that night.

The feeling in the room was intense as the guests watched the two of them, and wondered, and hesitated. What did they see? Perhaps Mary poured the ointment over his head in the way it was often done, and then — on impulse and remembering that other woman — poured the rest over his feet, and shaking loose her bound hair, wiped them with the long locks of it. Or perhaps the vivid memory of that earlier story became associated in the minds of the onlookers with what they saw. Or was that indeed what they saw, whereas Matthew and Mark's accounts, depending on second-hand reports, took a more conventional action as the more likely? The truth of it, the outpouring of love and grief and compassion, was in Mary's heart and in her hands, as they touched him, tenderly and with reverence, and it was in the heart of Jesus as he felt that touch and understood its message, the sharing and yearning in it, the unspoken promise of constancy which was hers but also that of all those women who through him had found freedom. She stayed there for a while beside him, saying nothing, for all was said, and her presence and her action were healing, balm on his body and on his spirit.

The enraptured silence did not endure, and as the two figures remained in quiet communion some of the guests moved restlessly, fidgeting and resentful, threatened and uneasy because of the bond they perceived, because of the peace that seemed to flow between the man and woman while their own minds were unpeaceful and afraid. So they began to mutter and complain, encouraging each other to end the situation and put the woman in her place. Her behaviour, they told each other, was a typical bit of feminine extravagance, futile and unpractical, it was intolerable that the Master should be subjected to such a display of hysterical emotion, more sensible counsels must be heard. He who constantly preached about concern for the poor would certainly admit that there were better ways to use money than to pour it all away. But somehow he seemed unimpressed by their remonstrances. The poor always call on our love, he told them, and such a reckless expenditure of love as this woman is showing cannot be confined. Let her alone, for what she has poured out continues to flow, what is lavished on the poverty and need of Jesus can never be denied to those he loves — the needy and the poor who are always to be seen by eyes accustomed to love. Let her alone, for once more she has chosen the best part. He knew in himself the power of the symbol, clarifying his own sense of purpose, strengthening him to face what lay ahead, while the power of love that spoke in the symbol brought new courage with the needed assurance of companionship. If it was an anointing for his burial, he knew that these his friends would not fail him, they would accompany him on the paths of death, and to burial with their anointed one.

They did not fail, they remained with him to the end, and to them came the first knowledge of their life's triumph over death. To some it came directly and to others by the swift telegraphy of women's friendship — a friendship which had deepened through all those months of a common service that few noticed or acknowledged. These women were not important to the rest except for practical purposes, and they were not much respected, as the reaction to their reports of resurrection show, but they were there when others were not. They were there in the sense of being physically present, even in the face of violence or family criticism or social ostracism, but they were also "there" in the sense in which Scripture evokes the presence of divine Wisdom herself — "In the sacred tent I ministered in his presence, and so I came to be established in Zion", in the heart of the people, "in the city he loved", the new Jerusalem. Mary might indeed have said, and the others with her, "I spread my fragrance like choice myrrh ... I was like the smoke of incense in the sacred tent". They were present in the heart of Jesus and in the heart of the people he was calling into being.

Time and again that vision has failed, as those called to be God's people find it impossible to conceive of a Christ who does not establish himself, and his church, by methods in accordance with the usual standards of success. Time and again it has forgotten the poor and the brokenhearted and the oppressed while its leaders played big-business with the powers of this world. And time and again it has been women — though not only they — who have listened and pondered in their places of isolation and contempt. They have perceived loneliness and need as once they perceived the need of Jesus himself, and responded to it in the same way, with a lavish recklessness that has provoked the same response: "How unpractical! How foolishly wasteful! Why don't they stay home and look decorative and keep house and support the men who understand reality and the ways of the world?" But they went where they were needed; like Wisdom herself they "took root in the people whom the Lord had honored," the neglected and abused and forgotten. They went where no one else dared and they were mocked as unpractical, and denounced as unfeminine. When their work succeeded the things they had created were, more often than not, violently taken over by church officials who "kept the purse and knew what was in it".

That capacity for focusing on essentials, undeterred by public opinion, is a gift the world needs. The woman with the ointment and her companions saw through the doubts and the false visions, not because they were holier than the men who were also disciples but simply because they perceived things from within, grasping the heart of the situation. They responded as they could to what they saw, not with complete understanding or extraordinary insight, but with a determination to remain faithful to the one thing they knew to be real, even if they could not make much sense of it, or defend it in argument, or see any hopeful outcome.

"Faith" was the word Jesus often used to describe what he perceived in the women who came to him. It is "Pistis-Sophia", Faith-Wisdom, an awareness rooted in the heart of reality, but reality known by love. From that root, and only from that root, can the tree of Wisdom grow, and bear fruit which is food for human beings, to nourish the whole person. So Wisdom can say at last, "Come to me, you who desire me, and eat your fill of my fruit."

No other fruit is worth having, and when Jesus told the irritated and contemptuous dinner guests to "let her alone" he was giving permission to Wisdom to grow in her own way. Wisdom is the "word spoken by the Most High", and it was his own spirit whom Jesus recognized in the heart of Mary, and of all those women who have understood why she did what she did, because they do it too, then and since.

In that group of women around Jesus, disciples of Wisdom, we encounter people who understood something they could not fully express except in their actions, for the religious language available to them did not correspond to the experiences they were having, anymore than it corresponded to the experiences Jesus was having. Jesus' actions, even more than his words, challenged, frightened, inspired and infuriated those who witnessed them. Sometimes we see him trying to find words to explain what he was discovering through actions he felt compelled to undertake, even thereby contradicting the assumptions he had been brought up to make. He sat down to dinner with a rabble of undesirable people, for instance, simply because they flocked to him, and he liked them and responded to them, outcasts though they were, people beyond the pale of acceptability. Having done so he found himself in a new and explicit relationship to them which became central to his preaching. The encounters with the Samaritan woman and with the woman who had a haemorrhage are examples of this pattern. He did things, because of something in him that perceived people in a way most others didn't, but then he had to explain the choices involved, to himself and to others. The woman who anointed him at dinner did something to which he responded; then he had to explain his response. That is the pattern and that is why it is often easier to perceive the essentials of his notion of human and divine reality through his actions than through his words as the evangelists reconstruct them. What we have in the gospels are his explanations only as they were understood and interpreted by hearers and followers, and some of them were not well understood.

The religious language of the culture was not adequate to express what Jesus was discovering, but he drew constantly on the prophetic tradition within it, especially that of the second Isaiah. This gave him the language he needed to begin to understand what he was about, and to free him to do what he felt himself compelled to do. But he was pushed inexorably further and further, for as he lived out the prophetic declarations he discovered more and more implications in them. Parables were his characteristic means of expressing the nature of the thing that drove him. They made imaginatively available the paradoxical, religiously ambiguous nature of reality as he experienced it under the compulsion of the life he knew within him, a life he must wrestle to make ever more actual, changing his world as it changed him.

This process of action springing not from principle but from some inner source, and describable only in terms of prophetic poetry, is one familiar to many women and to those men — artists and prophets such as George Fox or Van Gogh — who are aware of drawing energy for their choices from some region inside themselves to which most cultural and religious language is irrelevant. They may learn also to find justifying formulae which satisfy the establishment of their time including their own internalized establishment, at least until such time as the contradictions become so glaring that accommodation is no longer possible, which is what happened to Jesus also. Then, as the history of the many sub-divisions of Christianity shows, they often try to create a new language, and a different way of life, which is obedient to the authority they have discovered within themselves, and have validated together with others who share the awareness. As a result they may leave the "parent" religious or cultural set-up, or it may expel them or suppress them, sometimes by killing or expropriating them, but sometimes by manipulating them into some kind of conformity. But even when they are suppressed the thing they perceived and expressed often finds a way to continue and grow in some form, and to re-emerge at a later date.

This is what happened to those earliest women who found themselves freed to choose by being put in touch with the authenticity of their own deepest desires and insights. They were healed, Luke says, of "evil spirits and infirmities," the imprisoning and distorting effects of the struggle to be a person when the culture's powerful depersonalizing processes laid layer upon layer of guilt and fear over the whole awareness of being female. They had been healed, and enabled to be servants as he was a servant, which meant to be equals and friends. They were, it seems, mainly middle-aged and middle class, mothers of grown-up children, in some cases. We know a few names — sometimes no more than names, as in the case of Joanna. Susanna was "the wife of Herod's steward," a fact which hints at a whole drama of the renunciation of a rich and luxurious court life. One was Mary, the mother of James and Joseph who were probably cousins of Jesus; if so she was his aunt. She may have been the sister of Jesus' mother, (though with the same name that seems unlikely unless they were half sisters) or else her husband, Alpheus, was Jesus' uncle, and brother to either Mary, the mother of Jesus, or Joseph. In any case there was close family connection. Salome, "mother of the sons of Zebedee", was also possibly a childhood connection. (Jesus and his mother and cousins had left Nazareth when it became too unpleasant for the family, and settled in Capharnaum, perhaps because they had relatives there). Simon and Andrew lived in Capharnaum; evidently Jesus later lodged with them rather than with his family. Simon's wife and mother-in-law were among those who knew him familiarly, and these two women may have shared in the development of one of the earliest "house churches" which gathered in their home, as early inscriptions attest. Or perhaps Simon's wife was travelling with him, as fellow missionary, as Paul suggests.

So some of these women knew each other well already, and were even related. They came from similar backgrounds, from simple, hard-working but not impoverished families having some property and local status. Others were from quite different backgrounds, like Martha and Mary who owned a house large enough to receive Jesus and a number of disciples, or Susanna with her court connections, or Mary the mother of John Mark, whose home became a gathering place for followers of Jesus after Pentecost. It may even have been the place where that happened, or the place of the Last Supper, or both.

There were, says Luke, "many others". Some of them provided hospitality for Jesus and his friends in their homes. They offered that much needed privacy in which could develop the deeper explorations of thought which were impossible in public preaching and so necessary to the growth of the disciples, and of Jesus himself. Sometimes we hear that conversations took place "in the house," and we realize it had to be somebody's house, and recognize also the kind of occasion that Luke describes, where the women were involved both as hostesses and as disciples, and conflict could easily arise. Those who travelled with Jesus, leaving their homes and families, "provided for him and his friends from their own resources" and they had to have places to do that, so we get a picture of a practical collaboration between the women who offered their homes, and those who moved around with the group. The matter-of-fact way in which Luke tells us that these women "followed him" is amazing, for they are thereby bracketed with the Twelve as people who had (in Mark's version) "left home or brother or sister or children or lands" for his sake. Evidently women did leave husbands if their discipleship made it necessary and it may be that Susanna was one of these. In some cases they were possibly widows, or the husbands were also believers, but the break with custom is none the less extraordinary, all the more for being mentioned without comment.

We are given little enough detail, yet that little is informative. In the first chapter I suggested that the attitude of women to the human body of Jesus was important. This is a thread that runs through the many stories about Jesus with women, and it is evident in Luke's reference to the fact that women "provided for them". It was a natural and traditional thing for the women's contribution to include caring for the physical needs of the party, and it is something women (and not only women) find satisfying. This bothers some women nowadays, because the role of "nurturing" has been made to seem inferior, a care for the "merely material", which is "all women are good for", but the women who experienced their discipleship at least partly by providing good meals were doing something fundamental, which Christianity has often lost sight of, and in doing so has lost touch with the Christ who expressed his sense of the meaning of "the kingdom" most often in action by assembling his motley collection of friends for a meal, and in words by telling stories about meals and banquets, and the guests who gathered at them. If we mean anything by "incarnation" the notion involves caring for bodies — feeding, healing and delighting in them.

The physical body of Jesus was the very heart of the message, the point where the inflow and outflow of life itself was experienced. His physical actions were often "feminine" actions of feeding and embracing, and healing — often by touch. The women focussed their awareness of him on his physical presence, often by-passing his words, which they could no more fully understand than the men. The story of the mother of James and John shows that sometimes, when they did think they understood, the women could make fools of themselves as readily as Simon Peter, or the "Sons of Thunder". But the action of anointing Jesus at the banquet was a statement of exquisite clarity and relevance, and displayed a deeper intuitive understanding which did not stop there.

These women were "with" Jesus, as a human bodily person. They floundered, as did the men, in trying to make sense of his role and status in terms of their religious background, but they clung to him as their savior, for that was what he was. They had listened not just to his words but to him, and they waited and pondered and shared their impressions and fears and half-formed ideas. So, finally, when the dreams collapsed and none of what they had hoped or expected was happening, there was still something left. There was still their sharply focussed commitment to himself, to his actual physical being, their very womanly love which could not be distracted from that essential point.

The men, who loved him just as much, were demoralized with fear and confusion because so much of their devotion had been built on the fragile foundation of Messianic expectations, and they simply had not been able to take in the warnings of Jesus himself, or the very obvious indications to which he pointed of what must happen when the hatred of the authorities and the disillusion of the people coincided. The men, also, were personally in danger of arrest, (the women at this stage were not) so their panic is understandable. The point is that the women, as a group, seem to have stayed as close to Jesus as they could get, not because they could do anything for him, or out of loyalty, or because they were more courageous than the men, but because it did not occur to them to do anything else. And after it was all over they stayed near the tomb and returned to it as soon as possible for the same reason. Apparently that was enough. That was all that was needed as a starting point for the proclamation of resurrection.

It is from this same point that women now are able to initiate change. Many are aware that, in all the confusion and fear and explanations and "solutions" for this time there is one essential central point, which is the kind of caring for one another that becomes possible among people who are freed from imprisoning categories and able to reach out without guilt and in spite of fear. This basic caring for persons as persons, thereby calling them out of oppression and deathliness, created the earliest churches and now holds the only hope for averting the doom which masculine-dominated secular and religious structures have made so extremely likely.

In those days Jesus announced doom, and announced an alternative. The women intuitively grasped the essential nature of the alternative, because they had themselves experienced that kind of liberation in their own bodies, through his body. The newness had to come from there, and it still has to. The coming together of people who can care for each other and learn the skills of caring for still others — skills of healing of body and mind, skills of caring for the earth from which bodies and minds grow — is still the way of the kingdom, the alternative to doom, but also, perhaps, the only possibility of another world beyond disaster. Jesus told his friends, "I am among you as one who serves," and the action by which he enforced that word was one of very basic bodily caring — the washing of his friends' dusty feet. This was not merely an acted metaphor for some more rarified kind of service. Rather it was what he called it — "an example". Wash feet, or sick bodies, heal, comfort. But also, feed people.

The Eucharistic action is first of all what women do, it is an act of feeding. The food to be shared must be prepared, it is a caring action. It is at the heart of the experience of caring for people just as people, beyond all social and religious categories. When Jesus had withdrawn from his friends the support of one kind of category, that of master and servant, he "did not leave them orphans". He gave them another, the relationship of people who sit around a table as equals and share food. This was the relationship he had experienced throughout his ministry as quite specially important, whether among the outcasts he gathered in his home, or among the wealthier, when they would receive him. This relationship John's gospel names for us — it is no longer that of servant to master, but of friends. Friendship is defined; it involves a willingness to give one's life for the friend, and a willingness to share even the deepest concerns, "all which my Father has revealed to me". It was at table that Jesus' friend came to him to share her understanding and her grief, and in some sense to accept from him the gift of his life on behalf of all those who wait in silent sorrow. It is no wonder, perhaps, that it was these friends, emerging from the shadows, who first perceived the Easter glory and shared it.

IV.
SINNERS

If the word "sin" is used in connection with a woman, everyone knows what it means. A sinful man may be a thief, an extortionist, a drug-dealer, a traitor, but a sinful woman is an adulteress or a prostitute; her sin is sexual. Women ... sex ... sin — they go together in the mind of our culture, even now, though the last word may be accompanied by a snicker and put in inverted commas.

This point has been made many times, and the long history of oppression which the equation justified is well known though not sufficiently well known. One vitally important fact emerges from the gospels, which is that Jesus did not use those categories, though he was expected to. He encountered many whom his society labelled sinners, including women marked as sexual offenders, but on no occasion did he address them as a special category, except in the sense that they belonged among those whose treatment made him angry, and for whom his compassion was stirred — the "little ones", the marginalized and oppressed. In his culture those referred to as "sinners" were not necessarily guilty of any moral offense at all, the description was more akin to a class distinction than a moral one. As we have seen, they were the ones who would never make it into religiously or socially respectable circles, because their work, their parentage, their health or their income made them in some way unacceptable to those who claimed the power to define who was in God's favor and who was not. In the eyes of the religious establishment, especially the Pharisees, those who did not maintain strict observance of the law, especially the laws of cultic purity, were sinners. So in considering the behaviour of Jesus with "sinful" women, we need first to look at how he dealt with "sin" in this sense.

The story of the healing of the paralysed man shows very well the way Jesus regarded "sinfulness", and it helps in understanding his attitude to "sinners", including women. He was faced with a barricade of law and custom which carefully excluded those regarded as unacceptable to God. The "sinners" themselves were often equally convinced of their hopeless reprobation. They were also, therefore, frequently sick in mind or body or both as a direct result of the guilt and anger and misery induced by their outcast condition. It was a vicious circle, since sickness or poverty was regarded as a divine punishment, thus reinforcing the sense of guilt beyond any purging. They had a sense of being permanently rejected by God, no matter what efforts they made. Neither wealth nor moral rectitude could change their lot, for often their wealth was regarded as "illgotten" and therefore could not be used for the necessary sin-offerings, and personal rectitude equally counted for nothing without the means to pay for re-instatement. Acceptability, moreover, was controlled by those whose sense of God-ordained power rested precisely in their superiority to the "rabble without the Law"; this included control of the means of forgiveness. It is not otherwise in most religious systems; the greatest power of any clerical or quasi-clerical system has always been in its control of consciences, by defining what is and is not sinful, and if and when and how forgiveness may be obtained.

The long history of infants abandoned or killed because their mothers would be irredeemably outcast if they were known to have borne a child out of wedlock is one example of the exclusion of "sinners" by a standard of morality which upheld the property and inheritance rights of the ruling and middle-classes, and excluded from the possibility of social or religious forgiveness those whose behaviour did not fit the pattern. The woman who "sinned" was permanently outcast (unlike the man in the case). If she kept her crime hidden she still carried a burden of guilt to her grave; if it were known, her fate was probably prostitution, or suicide. The situation now is not very different — prostitution is still frequently the fate of girls who have been sexually abused. The shameful history of manipulation of penitents in confession in the Catholic tradition is another example, and in particular the trap of guilt and helplessness into which divorced Catholics are caught, but other churches and sects operate the same systems; the public denunciation and humiliation of sinners (mainly women) in the nonconformist Chapel tradition, is still a recent memory. The feeling that only "good" people go to church is still as strong as ever, and it is not even necessary to exclude the "sinners". They exclude themselves, with just the same feelings of inevitable unworthiness that "sinners" felt in the time of Jesus.

The paralytic in Capharnaum was one of these, a person literally paralysed, his physical condition reflecting and resulting from his spiritual paralysis. His was the total apathy of one who knows he cannot move, has no choices that mean anything, since others control his destiny and he has given up trying. He could do nothing for himself, but in this case he had friends who could do something. The solidarity of outcasts often amazes social workers and police, and the ingenuity and persistence of these friends won the admiration of Jesus immediately. The man may not even have wanted to be helped, it was an example of that loving substitution which is the essence of salvation — "he saved others, he cannot save himself", and we all save each other and are saved in and by each other. "Jesus saw *their* faith", and it was enough, and his response went to the heart of the matter, "Your sins are forgiven." He is not remembered as saying, then or at other times, some such form as "I forgive you," or even "God forgives you". The implication by the evangelist is rather that he acts as a catalyst, releasing in the person the awareness of being forgiven which has been, as it were, locked in — paralysed — by the conviction of guilt.

There is an interpolation in Mark's gospel, awkardly inserted to clarify the meaning, which reads "but so you may know the Son of Man has power on earth to forgive sins." It is syntactically awkward, put in to make a point, and it expresses the young church's conviction about the redemptive role of the Christ. But the scene is complete without it. The Pharisees and scribes, the guardians of the status quo, were incensed that this man, not content with healing bodies, was publicly calling into the select circle of the acceptable a person whom their laws had excluded. "Who can forgive sins but God alone?" But they were the ones — they alone — who decided whether or not God forgave. And Jesus was throwing forgiveness around as if it were free, and available to all without distinction.

Once this man was convinced that he was no longer fixed, that he could make choices, could move from the outside to the inside of the area of God's acceptance, he moved indeed. To tell him to take up his sleeping mat and walk was merely to demonstrate, to the man himself and to the spectators, the nature of what had already happened. In the thought of Jesus healing and forgiveness are not separable, they are aspects of the same self-discovery as a whole person, free to move, to choose, to love. So Jesus' call to "repentance" is a call to recognize the possibility of this wholeness, the possibility of choosing to come out of apathy and guilt and claim the reality which was always there, but was locked in by the sense of sin and rejection. The "sinner" is one who has left home, so all the prodigal has to do is come back home, where the child has a right to be, even if she or he has come to feel that right has been lost. And this right is unconditional and inclusive, in the words and actions of Jesus. But this is an attitude which the religious establishment of his time, and later times, has been unable to tolerate. In their eyes, there have to be limits and conditions. How can anyone be "in" except in contrast to those who are manifestly "out"?

Jesus' basic attitude to sinfulness, then, was that it didn't have to be, and that people should walk out of that man-made prison as quickly as possible, and then set about calling others out also. This was the most subversive aspect of his behaviour, the one which most throughly persuaded the authorities that he must be got rid of.

It was an attitude which he adopted at an early stage, but it developed and grew, and one of the most striking incidents in the four gospels is the one in which Jesus was confronted with what was, for a Jew, the most fundamental exclusion of all, that of pagans. There were sinners in Israel, but their outcast condition was as nothing to the total unacceptability of the uncircumcised, the idolators. That the pagans were unclean and rejected was the basis on which the people of Israel knew themselves chosen and holy. National chauvinism is not merely a Jewish phenomenon. The intellectual snobbery of the French, the smug ignorance of the British, the brassy arrogance of the Americans are only examples of a universal tendency to put down foreigners. Over and over again the prophets had called Israel to open its gates and heart to the nations but, whatever the prophets had said, dislike of Gentiles was such a fundamental aspect of everyday Jewish feeling of that time that there was no need even to think about it. In the story of the Syro-Phoenician woman, (a Greek, says Mark, to underline her pagan and foreign condition) we find that Jesus assumed, as the prophets had done, that the mission of Israel was to call nations to holiness, yet that the benighted condition of the heathen would necessarily make that a very tough assignment. In his mind, therefore, the prerequisite was the conversion of Israel itself, which would then take the message of salvation to the nations. His own primary task was to call "the lost sheep of the House of Israel" to a sense of vocation.

This Greek woman, then, represents the pagan world, not as an abstraction, but in a human encounter in which the Jewish assumptions were challenged by the reality. Jesus was in foreign territory at the time, at least partly because Israel was showing itself slow to hear the message of forgiveness and hope, and he was exhausted, harassed, and in need of time to rest and think at a distance from all that. He stayed, it seems, in Jewish households in that country — he was in a house, presumably a Jewish house. (He would not have entered a pagan one, for his starting point in this matter as in others was that of the traditional Jewish faith with its unquestioned beliefs and assumptions. The difference in him was that at every turn he was able and willing to look at the significance of experiences which brought those assumptions in question when they were contrasted with the central, overwhelming fact of his experience — that of a God who is loving and merciful, who looks at the heart, not at behaviour or status.)

Jesus had crossed over into Gentile territory at a point in his public career and in his personal development at which the conflict with the ruling establishment had become significant. The lines of battle were drawn. His hopes of winning over the rulers of Israel by the simplicity and clarity of his message, and the enormous compassion which gave it urgency, had faded. Many who had followed him no longer did so, and though the "little ones" were his to the end, they were "harassed and helpless", too accustomed to being pushed around to be able to grasp the possibility of change in a lasting and practical way.

It is possible that the tour through the regions of Tyre and Sidon and the Decapolis took place in the period following the decisive confrontation in Jerusalem, the "Palm Sunday" episode which is generally associated with the passion story, because Matthew and Mark place it, for dramatic reasons, in that context. But the entrance into Jerusalem and the cleansing of the Temple probably came some time before, and John's gospel puts the Temple incident quite early in his ministry. It seems natural to see it as the climax to his Galilean popularity, and his espousal of the cause of the "little ones", who followed him, triumphant and cheering, into the Temple, and with him cleared it and claimed it as their rightful heritage. John also draws for us a picture of the type of acrimonious and dead-end confrontation with the authorities in the Temple which rose to such a pitch of incomprehension and bitterness that Jesus was forced to withdraw from the city in order to avoid violence to the ones for whose sake he was there. Such a rejection and withdrawal, after a decisive statement of his intention and a period of apparently successful "take-over" of the Temple court on behalf of the people, must have necessitated deep and painful reflection on the future course of his ministry. It may well be that his apparently aimless travelling in unfamiliar territory gave him the time he needed for prayer and pondering and sharing of experience with his friends. He was feeling his way into a different and stranger sense of direction, one later illumined and confirmed in the experience of transfiguration on the mountain.

We may, in any case, see in the journey a time of retreat and reflection during which no publicity was expected or wanted. He was there as a private person, staying in Jewish homes, among people who knew little or nothing of his public career, since in the days before newspapers his face was not known to them, and his name was a common one. Yet even there he could not always be perfectly anonymous. There were people who had travelled or visited, or had been on pilgrimage to Jerusalem, who brought back stories of the popular and controversial preacher, and spread them not only among the Jewish inhabitants but, by gossip at the well or in the market, to the Greek population of the towns also.

The Syro-Phoenician woman, whose little daughter was tormented with some severe sickness of the mind, heard the stories and sought him out. Even a rumor of healing power was enough to inspire her to take the risk of pursuing him, though she knew he would probably despise her as a woman and a heathen. Distraught as she was with the daily misery of her child's suffering, she would at least try. It is interesting that she tried to make her appeal more impressive by addressing him as "Son of David", a title alien to her but perhaps picked up from the stories she had heard. The "Hosanna to the Son of David!" of the Jerusalem crowds was recent and being talked of.

Jesus did not answer her first cry for help and his strange silence suggests that this violation of the privacy he sought, and the form of it, roused bitter memories. He only wanted, at first, to avoid what her cry called him to. Would the misery of the "little ones" never cease to press upon him? He had raised such hopes, and had been forced to withdraw, causing disillusion and bewilderment and anger. Now, in this foreign place, he was still pursued by the thing that he had always been unable to resist, the pathetic hopefulness of the outcast, the sinful, the ones nobody cared for.

"Send her away", his followers begged. She was a nuisance, still crying out, pleading, clutching, making a fool of herself and a public show of them. There is no question in their minds of listening to her plea; if the heretic Samaritan woman was unacceptable to them, this woman was even more so. She was outside consideration, not because they were callous but because their imaginative sympathies, though sharpened by the example and teaching of Jesus in relation to "the lost sheep of the house of Israel", simply did not extend beyond them. But the compassion of Jesus was not a learned thing. It was the driving motive of his life, and the woman's foreignness made her plight all the more poignant. Her obstinate hopefulness was a torment, and he defended himself against it with anger and yet half-humorously.

"It is not right to take the children's bread and give it to the puppies. Let the children first be fed," and as he said it he remembered how the children had refused the food. That bitterness explains the initial unkindness. There is also perhaps a sense that something in her face and attitude made him challenge the woman. Here was the mother of a child with a severe mental illness, who had suffered all that goes with that of discouragement, guilt and isolation; yet she had not lost her courage, her love, or her hopefulness. Perhaps the bitterness of his response reflects the depth of his awareness of her quality. This outcast, polluted, "heathen" woman possessed something which he, in that moment, needed, and her response to him conveys just that. Unabashed, sure that her love could somehow penetrate the barriers of Jewish pride which was no novelty to her, she answered him in kind. She picked up his image, yet changed it profoundly. He had pictured hungry children deprived of food in order to feed dogs; her picture, drawn with the humor of a mother who knows how children behave at table, shows the children not very hungry, sharing their unwanted food with the puppies who are, after all, also a part of the household. Her intuitive awareness of the pain behind his reaction, even interpreting perhaps some of the rumors of his recent rejection, gave her the words not only she, but he, needed.

It was brilliant and beautiful communication of compassion, and it liberated him. "Great is your faith!" A "thank you" is surely evident in that response. "For this saying", as Mark has it, "go your way. The demon has left your daughter." It could not be otherwise. Again, he does not claim a private power to heal or forgive, but rather unlocks the merciful power which has been restricted by fear or ignorance. "Be it done as you desire", for the passion of love is stronger than discouragement, in the woman, but also in Jesus.

That same passion of love is evoked in the peculiar little story of the woman caught in the act of adultery, which has been inserted sometimes in Luke's gospel, sometimes in John's. It floats, homeless, while scholars argue about where it should fit, and yet it insists on being part of the New Testament, it will not go away. In this it is typical of the curiously unintegrated quality of several of the references to women in the gospels, as if the male writers were burdened with these names and incidents and could not get rid of them without violence to the yet-young tradition, but did not know how to deal with them. The story of the adulterous woman is not possible to place chronologically with precision, but as it stands it is located by the writer in the Temple at a time when Jesus was teaching openly there, and it seems possible that it belongs among the several accounts of the attempts by doctors, Pharisees, "chief priests", and others to discredit Jesus and dislodge him from the security of the people's affections, which constituted an obstacle to the authorities' desire to "do away with him". Since he was known for his tendency to favor sinners, it seemed a useful gambit to try to show up Jesus as one who rejected the Law and its final authority, Moses, and therefore no fit leader or teacher in the eyes of good Jews. If, however, he did in fact uphold the necessity of a death penalty for adultery, he could be accused of rebellion against Rome, since Rome reserved to itself alone the right to punish by death.

The purpose of the confrontation, therefore, was to discredit Jesus; the woman was merely a convenient tool. The revulsion of Jesus at the whole proceeding is eloquently shown by the action described — he simply refused to have any part in a maneuver that for sheer petty nastiness exceeded any of the other little traps they had devised. He was teaching at the time, sitting down as was usual. He did not move, he merely bent down and began tracing patterns in the dust. The accusers, prepared for his renowned acuteness in debate, were non-plussed by this silence, and could only go on repeating accusations which sounded less impressive with each repetition, as the indignation and enthusiasm they had worked up found nothing to work upon. As for Jesus, he went on drawing. He needed, perhaps, a short time to deal with the mixture of compassion, contempt and grief which their horrid little game provoked. He who had wept over the blindness of Jerusalem saw before him the proof of precisely that refusal to see the reality of the God which Jerusalem claimed to serve. There was only a desire for power and control and an indifference to the suffering of the weak.

The law required those who brought an accusation to carry out the sentence. When Jesus finally raised his head to look at the eager accusers he did not ask them to be merciful, but only to uphold the spirit, as well as the letter, of the Law they claimed to revere. It was necessary that those who proclaimed another person sinful should do so out of a clear conscience, or else their witness was questionable. Could these would-be eradicators of sin claim to be free of it? "Let the one without sin cast the first stone."

The context suggests that he was not asking them whether they were perfectly righteous, for such a demand would be unreal and uncharacteristic. What he was asking was whether they counted themselves free of guilt in the area in which the woman herself was accused. They had accused this woman of indulging illicit sexual passion — had they never done the same? If this reading is correct then we have here a quite new equation — sexual misbehaviour in a man is as blameworthy as in a woman. Such a thought was indeed amazing to the men of the time, and most times, but not amazing to Jesus, who did not deal in categories that regarded as acceptable in one person what was worthy of death in another. But the men who had accused the woman belonged to a group exclusive enough and public enough for its members' behaviour to be known, at least within the group. Preposterous as the implied suggestion was, each one was driven to remembering the occasions on which he had visited prostitutes, or taken advantage of a servant girl, and each could not but know that others would also remember; some of them had probably talked about these exploits to each other, compared notes, laughed over their "conquests". But somehow, faced with that angry, grieving face, they could not laugh anymore. He bent again to his scribbling and there was silence. First an older man, perhaps a man of sincerity and of more tender conscience, turned and gravely went away, driven to a new degree of self-knowledge. With that, the position of the others became less tenable. They looked at each other, coughed, fidgeted, muttered something or other, and slipped into the crowd as unobstrusively as possible. Even the bystanders drew back, sensing the tensions, and the woman was left standing.

Jesus sat up and looked at her, and this time it was different. This time it was just two people together. His glance at her showed him her misery, her shame and humiliation; this was not a time for much talking, only for the simplest kind of reassurance. He spoke as if to a child, gently helping her to realize that the ordeal was over. "Where are they? Has no one condemned you?" "No one, sir" — her own whispered words shaped the assurance she needed — they had really gone. "And I'm not condemning you either," he told her. You are free to go — free, do you understand? You are free to choose, to be your own person. "Do not sin again," do not be driven, deprived of choice by the misery of your situation, escaping from one man's domination to the domination of another who cares for you, perhaps, as little. There is another way.

The woman disappears from our knowledge, as do all the other women in the gospels. Did she return to a marriage she hated? If she did, was she able to transform it? Did she, then or later, choose to follow the one who had given her freedom? The survival of this story is itself evidence that it was important to the earliest witnesses, and it is possible that the presence of the woman in one of the early communities was a reason for its preservation. If the woman became part of the Johannine church, this would explain why a story with a synoptic flavor floated into a Johannine context. But this is guesswork. What we do have is one more piece of evidence of the way Jesus dealt with contemporary attitudes to women. Even now, the difference in his approach is hard to describe because he consistently evades categories. We see him relating to a person in a horrible situation with directness and honesty and realism. All the usual issues — whether or not she was "really" guilty, the degree of responsibility, all the paraphernalia of moral theology, ancient and modern — are simply not addressed at all. We can't even find in Jesus an advocate for specific changes in the status of women, or in marriage law or custom, because those questions don't arise. In his vision of relatedness you don't just change rules or juggle with hierarchies; rather, the practical details of behaviour between human beings are totally governed by the fact of the Father's tender love for each person, in each person and between persons. Changes in custom, expectation and law follow.

The most famous story of Jesus with a sinful woman is the one already touched on, the story which became so closely entwined with the incident of the anointing at Bethany. In it we saw another example of the same attitude, and it was shocking and incomprehensible, not so much because a sinner was arbitrarily forgiven but because Jesus seemed to be saying that the forgiveness was in some way effected by the sinner's capacity for loving. In this scene Jesus once more used words which have become familiar. "Your sins are forgiven — your faith has saved you". What he did was release in the person the capacity for wholeness which had been obscured and denied by misery, guilt and fear.

There is an unmistakable implication in this story that the woman's capacity for becoming whole and free had come to birth before she came into the dinner party, possibly from a previous encounter with Jesus, or at least from hearing his message of compassion and hope for the outcast. Her behaviour towards Jesus was not so much a plea for forgiveness as evidence, to him, that the healing and freeing had already happened. It was the outpouring of a person almost beside herself with relief and gratitude, to whom social conventions were irrelevant, because nothing mattered but to find some way to express the greatness of the liberation to which he had called her. "She has loved much", so everything that kept her indebted is done away. "You are forgiven. Your faith has saved you." She needs that assurance, the solemn proclamation of her freedom. "So now go in peace," in the wholeness of a real person, free from labels and the man-made categories which have kept you in subjection.

But there are details in this story which are different from the other incidents described in this chapter. It spells out certain things which in the others are only implied. First of all Luke here underlines a contrast between the behaviour of his host and that of the woman, and it is in line with other occasions in which Jesus contrasts the sinner and the one who regards himself as righteous. The parable of the Pharisee and the Publican says it one way, and the accent in that parable is on the actors in it. The publican, heartbroken, yet turning to God, is very like the woman, sobbing at Jesus' feet, and Simon, the real Pharisee, is very like the Pharisee in the little tale — observant, sincere, giving due thanks, generous above the ordinary, yet lacking that passionate neediness which is the obverse of genuine compassion. But the parables of the lost sheep and the lost coin take the spotlight off that which is lost and keep the attention on the seeker. The seeker is God, and this God is extravagantly concerned for something which love sees as intrinsically valuable. To let it go, to write it off, is unthinkable, but that is just what Simon expected Jesus to do with that woman. If he did not, it must be because he was ignorant of her true character, and his ignorance was itself a condemnation — he couldn't be what he claimed to be. Righteousness, in this kind of thinking, is proved only in contrast to the unrighteousness which it repudiates. But, for Jesus, God's righteousness consists precisely in the refusal to repudiate anyone at all, indeed consists in the anxious and anguished maternal care which is expended for the sake of those least able to care for themselves. So the whole incident is a demonstration of what Jesus thought God's priorities and attitudes to be — as he knew and experienced them as his own driving motive and energy. Something happened to the woman and to Jesus. There was a mutual discovery, and that mutuality is itself the presence of God. This is indeed the one who, as the guests at the table wondered and muttered, "even forgives sins", because something is unlocked and the sinfulness ceases to exist. Like the paralyzed man, this woman could get up and walk, going from that house "in peace". She was whole, because she had poured herself out. The witnesses felt, as most people do, that personal integrity depended on a highly organized defense system intended to keep dangerous others in subjection and at a distance. Jesus' notion of integrity lay in the ability to shed all defenses, and so be at peace.

Another thing Luke suggests is also familiar. The frequently misinterpreted little parable in the middle of this story tells of two debtors owing very unequal amounts, and both "forgiven" their debts. Simon, rather reluctantly, concedes that the one with most reason for gratitude would be the one who owed the most. Jesus applies this to the woman who was indeed deeply in debt, and is therefore overflowing with loving gratitude because her "debt" has been wiped out. (The use of the idea of a cancelled debt in itself shows how Jesus thought of sinfulness as an artificial and unnatural situation which should be wiped out and forgotten.) The usual interpretation, that she was forgiven because she "loved much" doesn't fit the story Luke uses. Rather she loves because she knows herself liberated. But there is an implication that the host and those like him are those who "owe little", at least in their own eyes. If there is a debt, they feel, it is trivial and they can pay it off anytime, they don't need compassion. In this particular instance the host had been moved and impressed by Jesus to the point of ignoring possible criticism by asking him to dinner, but he hadn't put himself out at all; he did the polite minimum but showed "little love". But, for Jesus, sharing a meal with people was important. He was not only personally hurt, he felt a deep wrongness in the tacit denial of the openness and equal sharing implicit in sharing food and table. His thought, too, was deeply imbued with the prophetic symbolism of the bounty and inclusiveness of God's table, which was violated by the cold formality of that dinner party. The woman, on the other hand—uninvited guest though she was—displayed the divine generosity abundantly, but she was able to do so because she had herself been willing to receive divine abundance.

In all this we see very clearly the vision of the kingdom as Jesus saw it. So often his inclusion of the poor and sick in his scheme of things is interpreted as the result of pity or mere kindness, the gesture of the strong toward the weak. Yet over and over we get the sense that *he* needed *them*. In his isolation he needed love, in his depression, he needed challenge, in his search for meaning he needed a shared experience of longing and hope. He found among the outcast — but especially among women — a response of gratitude which was not servile but sensitive to him, open to what he had to give and wanting to give in return. This is why his attitude to "sinfulness" (however we define it) is so important. Those who have been imprisoned are best able to liberate others. The recovered alcoholic is the one who can pull another alcoholic out of despair; the therapist has to have been through the agony of self-discovery. The women who have found a freedom to be human are those who can reach out not only to imprisoned women but to men also. It was not accidental that women carried the Easter message, nor is it accidental that so many of the women shown to us in the gospels are outcasts — the woman in the Temple, the one in Simon's home, the Syro-Phoenician woman, the Samaritan woman, the woman with a haemorrhage, and also some of the women who are a little more than names, "who had been healed of evil spirits and infirmities". Through him they experienced the reality of themselves, there was compassion between them and their healer, and they became capable of releasing the divine power in others by their own compassion.

In all this healing and liberation, all this forgiving and loving, there is never a hint that women constitute a special problem by reason of their sexuality. They are neither dangerous, nor pitiable, nor exciting in that particular way. Later attitudes were to transform the great apostle Mary Magdalen into a kind of archetypal (sexual) penitent, because it gave men a thrill to think of a "bad" (meaning sexual) woman around Jesus. In order to do that she was identified with the sinful woman in Simon's home, but there is no evidence for such an identification. All it shows is the curious need of "spiritual" writers to bring in female sexuality and repudiate it by showing Mary as permanently penitent for her sexual lapses. Needless to say, none of the male disciples carry this aura of being excitingly suspect, yet safe because penitent — not even Matthew who was a tax collector and came from a very dubious background. There are no legends about Matthew spending the rest of his life in penitence. Only sexual sin attracts such expectations and only women are surrounded with it. Jesus, it seems, didn't have that feeling at all. In the only recorded instance in which he talked about sexual sin it had to do with men, their sexual acts and their fantasies about women.

In this context it is helpful to notice also that when Jesus talked about divorce he was talking about the rights of women to be regarded as fully human. He was speaking in the context of a culture in which women were the possessions of their husbands and could be disposed of like other property, for adequate reason. The only dispute was about which reasons were adequate. Mark, writing in Rome, expanded Jesus' prohibition of divorce to include a woman who divorced, because Roman women did have that right, within limits. But his expansion distorts the original intention, for it is clear that what Jesus was addressing was an oppressive situation in which women could be deprived of home, children (the children were the husbands' property also) and reputation, without redress. His denunciation of the "hardness of the heart" which the Law was designed to accommodate is perfectly in line with his denunciation of other forms of oppression of the helpless and needy people in power. "What God has joined" are not only husband and wife but human society, established by God in a covenant of mutual service. The care and support of each by each was what the Law had attempted to embody, protecting the right of aliens, widows and the poor to at least the basic essentials of life. There are passages in the Law which are amazing in their detailed concern not only for the survival but for the dignity of the weaker members of society. Even the animals are to be treated with fairness; the ox which draws the threshing sledge must not be muzzled — he has a right to the odd mouthful of grain in reward for his hard labor. The widows and orphans are to be guaranteed at least the corners of the fields, the wheat dropped by the reapers, the olives left on the tree after the first beating. But the Law itself, intended to protect the vulnerable, had become an instrument of oppression and control. It had little to say, in any case, on behalf of women, unless they were widows. When Jesus spoke out on behalf of married women he was once more saying something very threatening to a masculine-dominated society. To say that one human being should not summarily dispose of another was only to echo the Law itself, but to extend that notion to married women — to make them distinct persons, in other words — was to threaten the foundation of society. The disciples, in response, were gloomily aware that a notion of marriage which required them to treat women as persons with rights and feelings might be more than a normal man could cope with. It is a sad irony that Jesus' concern for the rights and dignity of women should have been turned into a means of controlling both men and women — but especially women — by levers of guilt and fear. Even today the abused wife is still often exhorted by spiritual guides to be patient in suffering rather than to seek freedom.

(Divorce as we conceive of it — a legal undoing of a contract which has somehow or other become an intolerable burden — was not what Jesus was talking about. What he might have said about that we may conjecture if we wish, but we cannot quote his words on divorce in support. They don't concern it. Perhaps we should look more to his sayings about compassion, and about the distortions which arise when Law is applied as an instrument of control.)

We have to conclude where this chapter began. To Jesus, women were simply people. They were of all kinds, and some had behaved with varying degrees of selfishness and irresponsibility in their sexual lives. Some had also no doubt been guilty of possessiveness, manipulation, self-pity or evil temper. But their sins were not in a special category. To him, the social labels attached to their failures were irrelevant, but he also knew what those labels could do to a person's sense of self. He knew, too, how a status of dependence often meant a loveless and even abused childhood followed by a loveless and abused wifehood, and the only escape from either could easily be to an equally loveless and abused career of prostitution. And his compassion but also his admiration were stirred when he saw women struggling against those conditions, able in spite of them to care, to love, to hope. In response he gave them the gift of themselves. He empowered them to become what they had it in them to be, because he saw it and believed in it himself.

V.
WHY WERE THEY FORGOTTEN?

When dawn broke over Jerusalem that morning after the Sabbath a new time began for all human-kind. The first heralds of good tidings to Zion were a group of women, mostly those middle-aged, middle-class mothers of grown up families whom we have already met. Theirs was the first Easter experience, they were the first to be sent with the news that was to change history. Why, then, when such a great and extraordinary part had been given to them in the drama of salvation, do we never hear of them again?

What we do know of these women apart from their appearance in the Easter stories is very little, as we have seen. The work of putting biographical clues together from the scanty material we have does at least give us the sense of being in touch with an identifiable group of people, but delving into texts for names and family networks is less important than trying to uncover the significance of the group as a whole, and especially of its relationship to the mission of Jesus, the spreading of the good news. Yet this proves difficult to do because there is an oddness about the gospel references to them, as if the evangelists found it necessary to include them but didn't quite know what to do with them. Matthew and Mark record the presence of women at the cross and at the burial, and so does Luke, clearly because that is the prelude to their arrival on the scene on Easter morning. John places three of them by the cross and Luke mentions them earlier in the context of the Galilean ministry, but without any special "story" to fit them into. One can imagine, for instance, a friend reading over Luke's manuscript of the resurrection and saying, "Who were they? How do they come into the story?" And Luke, who had the records of the answers to his "diligent enquiries", as well as the various other sources he drew on, mentally scanned, as it were, the huge "group photograph" in his mind of the hundreds healed and touched and converted by Jesus, and saw a few faces stand out because he knew them already in the more startling context of the Easter stories. So he recorded their earlier presence and a few of their names, yet the placing of the reference is arbitrary; one feels he could have put them in almost anywhere, for they were constantly there, from Galilee to Jerusalem and beyond.

They were constantly there, and "constant" is the best word to describe the little group. They were there, and they would not go away, and they are still there in those stories of the morning whose events have formed the heart of Christian preaching ever since. They are embedded in the Easter proclamation, acclaimed and glorious messengers. Yet, after that moment, we never hear of them again, with the possible exception of the unnamed "other women", with Mary the mother of Jesus, who waited and prayed with the rest before Pentecost.

There is a strange contradiction here. The early churches knew those stories of the first witnesses of resurrection, and all four evangelists use them in different ways, John concentrating on Mary of Magdala. After that there is silence.

Yet it seems very unlikely that after the healing and liberating, the years of active ministry for and with Jesus, they suddenly went home and settled down meekly to cook soup for their grandchildren. People like that do not just go away, yet as far as the records go that is just what they did.

In order to understand this strange juxtaposition of honor and oblivion we need to get in touch with the Easter experience, from the point of view of the women, and then of the men, for they were very different. It is important to remember that the women's point of view is the only one on which stories of the events of that morning could be based. The message was carried by the women alone; no one else saw or claimed to have seen divine messengers, or to have encountered the risen Lord at that time, and near the tomb. The stories of appearances to others place them much later in the day, or on later days. On the other hand the women's "point of view" is not known to us directly but only through the minds and expectations of the young churches and the male writers who wrote for them. It is interesting that some modern scholars have had trouble with precisely that part of the Easter story, and have speculated that the stories of the empty tomb were created in order to add force to the accounts of the disciples' experience of the risen Lord. By implication, then, the women's experience is invalidated. Others have suggested that the stories reflect liturgical celebrations held at the tomb by the early Jerusalem church. Perhaps the need these scholars have felt somehow to dispose of the evidence of the women gives us a clue to the similar difficulty which faced the male leaders of the young church when they were putting together a coherent account of their faith in order to present it to enquirers. What were they do do with the women's stories, for which there was no independent testimony? After all, a woman's uncorroborated witness was valueless in Jewish law.

We need to remember once more that the accounts we have come to us through the minds of writers who were sensitive, intelligent and honest, but none the less conditioned by their culture and its prejudices and expectations, which faith modified, but only slowly and partially. And the cultures of the time — Jewish or Gentile — gave little importance and less credence to women. These men had to deal with stories which had become part of the "faith story" and were known to many, yet did not fit their expectations at all. Through these accounts, can we still touch the root of the experience and begin to understand what happened? It is always risky to attempt to reconstruct gospel events, and some consider it naive even to try, yet we are dealing with human experience, however indirectly it reaches us — the experience of human beings who were where they were only because of a quite extraordinary constancy.

These were women who had given over their lives to Jesus because to each of them he had come as the liberator, the one who released some of them from sickness but all of them from the status of non-persons. They had inherited what Paul later called "the glorious liberty of the children of God". Jesus had broken open the categories of their servitude and their world was changed. But that change at once cut them off from the support systems of their society. They could not claim the freedom he gave them to follow, to be disciples, and at the same time live within the expected feminine roles, with their compensating securities as well as their humiliations. Paradoxically, the freedom they found was an isolating thing, as indeed it is for all disciples. Their old friends, neighbors and relatives were uncomprehending, puzzled and unhappy or openly hostile, as were those of Jesus himself in some cases. Even the male disciples with whom they lived and worked and for whom they cared were not entirely accepting, finding it hard to relate to them in any but the ways they had always related to women. The companionship in mission which we can discern in Paul's letters was not yet; these women disciples were a group apart within a group apart. But, perhaps all the more because of that, they were a group, not a collection of individuals, and they could support each other.

We have already imagined them, at those times when the Twelve had gone off somewhere with Jesus, or in the nights in their sleeping places, talking together, exchanging thoughts and experiences, deepening both faith and friendship. Their feelings and hopes were not necessarily those of their male friends and fellow disciples at all points, though they shared so much. One difference we have noticed is that their expectations were not focussed as completely as those of the men on a clearly defined Messianic triumph. No doubt they, too, believed that he was the one who should "restore the kingdom to Israel," yet when that hope crumbled they did not. Their constancy rested on something else, something which drew them even to the foot of the cross.

These were women who had in some cases come to know Jesus as he touched them physically in their need, and to others he had long been a familiar presence, before he became known to them as teacher and healer. In any case their love was focussed on his human presence, the concrete reality of his being, and the teaching they heard and treasured was known in its relation to that very personal relationship which they had with him. Whatever strange and marvelous identity might be attributed to him, whatever glorious future might be expected, it was not to that identification or to that future glory that the women constantly turned, but simply to himself. It was to this real person, rather than to any particular expectation of him, that they were constant.

They remained constant as doubts and fears and arguments rose and surged about them. No doubt they, with all his friends, were frightened and disturbed by the accusations of the religious authorities, to which they were even more vulnerable than the men. They too heard the murmurs of the fickle crowd, they were torn by the conflicting claims of their families and their Master, they felt the mounting tension among the Twelve as the sun of popularity disappeared behind the clouds and the storm threatened to break. Yet somehow the storm was not within. If they felt the cold blast of fear and confusion which finally daunted even those who loved Jesus best, it did not drive them away from him but towards him. Though they were on the margins of the action when the final drama began they drew nearer and nearer, and would not go away. They waited among the crowds outside the Praetorium and heard the murderous yells, and still they stayed. They were still there to follow the executioners' procession through the gates. They came nearer still; physically and spiritually they stood by the cross, as close to the one they loved as the soldiers would let them come. They were there with John, some permitted to stand even at the foot of the cross, some forced to wait a little further off.

They stayed there until the end and after. They watched the crowd melt away, its curiosity changed to superstitious fear, and still they waited, not willing to leave the body of the dead, because to them it was not just a corpse, a thing, but himself, the Master they loved If the soldiers had tried to put the body of Jesus in the criminals' common grave. as the custom was, it seems likely they would have had to battle with some very determined and passionate women. But an influential man obtained permission to bury the body in seemly fashon, if in haste.

Scholars argue about the burial, because the synoptic gospels say that the body was simply wrapped in a burial cloth and laid in the tomb, while John says that Nicodemus brought a large quantity of myrrh and aloes which were used for the burial. It seems odd in that case that the women later brought more, but perhaps the hastiness made it seem necessary to them to tend the body more carefully. In any case it was unthinkable to stay away. That is the foremost impression we get from the different accounts. They had been with him and they did not want to leave him. They could no more make sense of what had happened than anyone could, but something drew them to stay with him as long as it was possible to do so, no matter how futile it seemed. Also, it was not dangerous for them to do so, for at that stage the women were still insignificant in the eyes of the authorities. (This changed later, when men and women alike were jailed in the persecution following Stephen's death, a detail which is an interesting indication of the recognized status of women in the new communities.) They took full advantage of that insignificance. They bought spices as soon as the Sabbath rest was over and set off even before dawn to go to the tomb.

The gospels differ in the details of what happened. The resurrection stories are uneven, short, even inconsistent, perhaps because the fact was so central that for a long time the stories seemed less important. How many women went to the tomb? How many angels did they see? Which of them met Jesus himself? How did they react? We can never answer such questions because the writers drew on different oral or written accounts and had different theological points to make. Again we have to remind ourselves that we are reading material written for churches far apart — Mark writing in Rome, Luke also for a Gentile audience, John possibly at Antioch or Jerusalem. They picked out details that seemed significant, from a number of different sources. Also, the writers were trying to convey the sense of an experience which was (unlike the passion narrative, for instance) quite impossible to convey in normal language. We talk glibly about "angels" yet the one thing we know about the experience of people who claim to have encountered the force of divine energy in that form is that it leaves them shaken, awed, often speechless with fear and the sheer strangeness of it. Something got through, the women knew what they had to do, but the experience itself was incommunicable. We get echoes, too, of varied reactions: of fear, of reverence and awe, of instant joy, reflecting perhaps their different temperaments, with Mary of Magdala always the leader, an impetuous non-conformist.

But they did not only encounter angels; according to Matthew they met Jesus himself, or at least some of them did, and that was quite different. The amazing thing is that this meeting, unlike that with the angels, is presented not as frightening or strange or dazzling, but as simply very joyful, charged with inexpressible relief and mutual love; he was, it seems, as glad to see them as they him. John tells us that Mary of Magdala knew him as soon as he called her by name, but in the Synoptics the women recognized him at once. He was the one they had always known, incredibly restored to them, and they wanted to touch him, to be near that body from which they had never wanted to be separated. He did not deny them, but then he gave them something more. He did not so much withdraw his presence from them as give it over to them. They were to be, as the messengers had already told them, the means by which those others whom he loved might receive that which they, the women, had always known, though obscurely, and which they now received to over-flowing — the gift of that deep awareness of his absolute being at the heart of themselves, which his visible, tangible presence made actual for them. They had this sense in common with their friend John, he who grounded faith so firmly in that which "we have heard, we have seen with our own eyes, have looked upon and felt it with our hands ... the word of life".

This was their faith, and it was unshakable. When the pinnacle of Messianic ambition collapsed, that remained, and upon this faith was the message grounded, "Go and tell my brothers ..." and they went, no longer searching for him or clinging to him, for he was with them.

They hurried back through the still-shadowy streets where the day was just beginning. (Did Joanna, wife of Herod's steward, persuade the others to go first to tell her husband, or friends at court who were secretly sympathetic, since Herod's palace stood right beside the gate through which they entered? Was that why they did not encounter Mary and Peter and John hurrying to the tomb? Mary had left them earlier, as John tells us, and her meeting with the Lord was still to come. We cannot know, but it seems possible).

But when those first evangelists came to where their friends sat plunged in grief and confusion, the message received its first rejection. It is not hard to imagine how the men felt. Their world was in ruins, their hearts were aching with intolerable fear and shame and hopeless longing. They were in a state common to people hit by sudden tragedy, going over the incredible events, asking themselves if it could have been different — if only we had known, if we had done this, said that — if only ... It was all so recent, their imaginations were still full of the hopes and visions of only three days ago, and those were the sharpest pangs of a misery that lay within them like a physical weight, bowing them down. Fear for their own safety kept them within locked doors, and they were together in a companionship without comfort. During that long Sabbath day the women had shared that silent pain, suffering as much in compassion for their friends as in their own sense of loss. Therefore, as they hurried back through the city their keenest joy must have been in the thought of the comfort and hope they were bringing. "Tell my brothers ..." they had been commanded, and tell they did, their words falling over one another in their eagerness and conviction.

Perhaps it is not surprising that the first reaction was disbelief. "The story appeared to them nonsense," says Luke, and the Greek word he uses has the sense of the delirious babbling of a sick person. In their depressed state, that is how the women's words might easily strike these men. But it was not long before Peter and John returned to confirm at least part of the tale — that the tomb was empty. Why did they still persist in disbelief? After all, they had known the women a long time, some were their mothers, sisters, aunts, cousins, many were older than themselves; sober, commonsensical, capable people, whom they had learned to rely on. Yet each of the different accounts preserves for us the record of their disbelief.

The reason for the rejection of the women's initial witness is perhaps linked to the reason for the disappearance of these same women from the surviving accounts of the early days of Christianity. (The official accounts, that is. Later legends, which could possibly be based on more than pure imagination, tried to fill the gap that Christians felt.) Their word was rejected at first simply because it was incredible, but that rejection was maintained because to admit that they might be right was to admit the failure of the others. If the Lord had indeed been raised where did that leave those who had deserted him? And here were the women who had stood by him, claiming to have seen angels, to have seen the Lord himself, and they had not. It was intolerable. The tender concern of the message, its reassurance, its longing, were lost on them. All they could feel was bitter humiliation and anger.

Later, even that same day, they were convinced, they learned to understand, they were comforted and healed. And they were sent out to carry the message. But so were the women, for the message they had been given was needed by others besides their sorrowing fellow-disciples. The whole city and the countryside around was full of people who had hoped in Jesus and had their hopes dashed. How could these bearers of good tidings remain silent? Indeed we can be sure they did not, for when Pentecost came there were, so Luke tells us, many more people wanting baptism than can be accounted for by the number of those who could possibly have heard that first day's preaching, let alone been converted by it. The ground had already been prepared by the women's evangelism. These were women tested and found true, entrusted with a message which they must carry, and the names of some became known with their message — Mary — Joanna — Susanna — Mary — Salome ...

But after Pentecost the public preaching began, and the gathering and organizing of the rapidly growing company of believers under recognized leaders. "Acts" refers to them as the Twelve and others associated with them. These, according to Luke's sources, were the guides and interpreters of the Way, charged with the care of those converted.

These men whom Luke writes about were the leaders whom the church of his time designated as such in its official memory. But that was at least twenty-five years after the event, even more if late dating of "Luke-Acts" is accepted. In that time the problems of the Jerusalem church with the role of women had had time to develop, and were dealt with by the exclusion of women from leadership. Luke, as we shall see, took for granted a real but quite secondary role for women, which parallel evidence from Paul's letters contradicts in a number of places. Luke accepted the model of church he found as the norm, and traces of the part played by the women in the early preaching in Palestine are almost obliterated. We can uncover a few, and the exciting process is an exegetical and hermeneutical detective story, too lengthy and technical to be appropriately dealt with here. (It is greatly complicated by the patriarchal bias shown in translations of Scripture.)

The point that I want to look at here is that whereas there are many, if ambiguous, references to the role of women in "Acts", none of those named is from the group which played so signal a role in the ministry, death and resurrection of Jesus as recounted in the four gospels. Why?

It is significant that the women whom the male leaders came to know in later ministry were encountered as leaders of house churches or as fellow missionaries, at a stage when the men's own faith had become strong and articulate. That was a very different experience from the first one when the men were still broken and weak and the women were strong and full of joy. Perhaps somewhere deep inside they could not quite forgive that initial humiliation, for there are some experiences so sore, so intimately shameful, that we cannot even bring ourselves to think of them, but often reject from our minds the persons associated with those memories. And the opportunity to rationalize all that was available in the normal social and religious expectations that women should be relegated to submission and insignificance. And Jesus was no longer there to challenge those tendencies, to call women to the center, to affirm their role as disciples and missionaries.

So, some twenty or more years later, when Luke was putting together material for his account of the early days of the church, questioning eyewitnesses and drawing on common records and memories, he came up against a silence about the women who had featured so gloriously in his own and other accounts of the resurrection. Did he meet any of them or hear of them? Some at least must have been still very much alive. Did he feel it tactful to say nothing, given a feeling among the leaders that this was a tricky subject? Or, most likely, did he himself feel that their part in the story was over and no more need be said, since they were clearly not prominent any longer?

Whatever the explanation, his own mind-set clearly did not question the relegation of women to generally passive and domestic roles as hostesses and supporters to the accredited apostles and teachers. He would not be likely to question the assumption that the women's role was secondary. There is an ambivalence in Luke's gospel. He mentions women with appreciation, includes the important incident of the affirmation by Jesus of Mary's discipleship, and tells us of the group of women who 'followed' Jesus — a term again referring to discipleship. But the women are supportive and separate, and it seems that he could not quite reconcile the stories which he found preserved with his expectations and his own later experience of the place of women in the church. He put them in his gospel conscientiously, because his sources gave them a place, and then left them out of the later story, because, in fact, that is where they were: out.

That attitude is certainly the one implicit in the way most of us learned the story of those early days. We learned to praise and admire the first messengers of resurrection but nobody suggested it was odd that they had, on scriptural evidence at least, no part in the further preaching of the good news.

We may, and should, begin to suggest that it is odd. The reasons for that omission are understandable both historically and psychologically, and we cannot blame our forebears for being people of their time, but in our time we are learning to go back to the roots of our faith in a different way in order to rediscover the calling of Christians. When we do that we encounter a group of women who were healed and called and who responded and continued to respond. The fact that their work has gone unrecorded does not excuse us from taking up the labor they first undertook.

There are many deeds recorded with approval in past centuries of the church which we now regard with loathing and shame — such things as the burning of witches and heretics, the massacres of Jews and the devastation of cities in the name of Christ during the crusades. We cannot whitewash the crimes of our ancestors (and sometimes we learn from them to reject such comparable actions as giving Christ's name to a nuclear submarine). But equally and more happily Christians have learned to acclaim people, deeds and ideas which the church once rejected or persecuted. In neither case are they untrue to the living tradition of faith in Christ, rather we affirm its power to survive even such distortions, for the gates of hell have not prevailed.

That is why women are trying, with a constancy worthy of their fore-sisters, to get in touch with something which has undoubtedly shaped the development of our faith but has seldom been acknowledged and often denied. Those women at the tomb were only the first of many Christian women whose message went unheard, yet who did not give up. It is true that some, accepting the current valuation of womanhood, did abandon the struggle. Some submitted to what they thought must be greater wisdom, some retired into bitterness, still others sought beyond the church to discover the truth which the church seemed to deny them — and these also we have learned to respect. But many did not give up and did not become embittered or alienated, even in the face of persecution. Mary Ward, imprisoned in Rome, comes to mind, and Teresa of Avila, who suffered from similar attempts to destroy her work. Margaret Fell and many other early Quakers spent long periods in prison, Ann Lee and other early Shakers were vilified and beaten and threatened with death. Indeed such treatment can almost be said to have been a routine part of new ventures in Christian living in which women were involved. (Not only women of course, but it was more threatening to find women taking radical initiatives and trying to live according to the gospel.) The records of the early days of groups of religious Sisters and other Christian women in America contain stories of compassion and courage and marvelous work, maintained sometimes in the face of implacable hostility from clergy who feared the achievement of these women. Some stooped even to defamation or blackmail to dislodge the women or destroy their influence, though others, to their honor, remained friends and supporters.

The story is old and it is not over, but the evil is part of the human situation. The courage and faith are the message of the gospel which can still emerge to bring light into dark places. The time has come to bring to light what has been hidden, to acknowledge openly the presence of the women. This time, when the stories are told, they will be told differently.

Women were the first witnesses of resurrection, and their work of evangelization has never ceased from that day on in spite of vilification and outright persecution. In breakaway sects women often found a role as preachers and ministers, at least until those that lasted long enough became respectable and in turn suppressed their women. One of the few movements that continued to treat women as full members of the church was the Society of Friends, and even they only just managed against a tendency in the eighteenth century to restrict the role of women. The Salvation Army and other nineteenth century groups and church societies allowed women greater scope, and the women used it to the point of causing alarm and despondency among their male counterparts. But they had to struggle for their limited freedom and defend it, not always successfully, even to themselves. The astounding thing is that the strenuous efforts made to eliminate women from any significant role in the churches — an effort involving every kind of strategy, including the manipulation of fear and guilt, fake romanticism, or sheer moral or physical bullying — never entirely succeeded. The underground movement of women who managed to hear Jesus' message of liberation and live it somehow continued. It is now coming out of the catacombs and becoming aware of its own energy and power — the power of compassion and of loving, of wholeness and hope.

VI. WOMEN TRANSFORMED

The popular coupling of the names of Martha and Mary derives mainly from the brief story about the sisters in Luke's gospel, which has been described earlier in this book. In this incident we see the claim of a woman to full and public discipleship vindicated over against the expectations that her role would be chiefly that of caring for the physical needs of the male. The later interpretation of the story, in terms of the contrast between the active and contemplative vocation, with Jesus on the contemplative side, has made the two names into symbols of the two kinds of women, the "doers" and the "be-ers", and there have not been lacking those who point out that while it was fine for Mary to be occupied with listening to Jesus, she and Jesus and the other men would have ended up very hungry if it had not been for Martha's "busyness". The purpose of this chapter is to make use of this apparent contrast and to examine the personalities of two real women and see that the matter is, as human beings are, considerably more complicated than this simple dualism suggests.

First of all there is a question about Mary herself. Which Mary? The Mary of Luke's story, Martha's sister, is "Mary of Bethany", clearly, and as such she is inseparable from her family — Martha, and Lazarus, her brother. But in Christian legend and iconography she has become confused both with Mary of Magdala, and with the "sinful woman" who anointed the feet of Jesus. The latter identification is a natural one, which I have examined earlier, but it led to the odd and otherwise inexplicable identification of a "sinful" Mary with Mary Magdalene. A novel was even written suggesting that Mary of Bethany was an errant young sister who had been rescued from a life of sin (in Magdala) by her encounter with Jesus, and returned home to Bethany. Such a reconstruction is just possible, though there is nothing to support it but the desire to explain the traditional, and very old, identification of the three (if there are three) women mentioned in the Gospels. The identification may have little to justify it historically, but it happened, and one likely reason for this is the fact, attested both by the canonical Gospels and by later gnostic and apocryphal Gospels, that Mary Magdalene was a person of great importance among the followers of Jesus, a woman of dominant personality, courageous, energetic, and unforgettable. This was the personality which in a sense absorbed into itself the less clearly defined character of Mary of Bethany and of the "woman who was a sinner" and it is with this person that I shall be mainly concerned, putting her alongside Martha, even though she was probably not Martha's actual sister. The Martha and Mary of Luke's story are not the basis of this enquiry, but rather the symbolic Martha and Mary, two kinds of women who left a strong but enigmatic mark on the gospel narratives. Yet the symbolic women are closely linked to the real ones.

The identification of Mary Magdalene with the sinner was consolidated by suggesting that the seven devils from which Luke says Jesus released her represent the depths of immorality from which she was rescued. This suggestion can find absolutely no basis in contemporary usage. The phrase clearly refers to what would now be called acute mental illness, and this is very important for women now.

A woman of outstanding gifts, sensitivity and strength, struggling to make sense of herself in a society which regarded her as a more or less useful or ornamental possession, was in the position of a prisoner. This is to some extent still the case. Indeed, one of the insights of feminist psychology has been that much (maybe most) mental and emotional illness in women has had its roots in the attempt to force women to fit themselves to male definitions of their personalities and feelings. Classical Freudian doctrine, defining closely and negatively what is "natural" for woman to be, and how she must conform herself to it or risk permanent emotional infantilism or mental illness, is only one of the more recent examples of this age-old horror. This kind of self-fulfilling prophecy is not new, for if the natural, God-given role of women is first defined by a patriarchal society then all deviations from it are bound to seem distortions. Most women, under heavy conditioning, conform to the expected role. A few will not; they either manage to break away and achieve a precarious and beleaguered autonomy, or else snap under the strain of the attempt, becoming mentally ill. In that state they join their sisters who, while willing and even eager to conform, are psychically unable to do so successfully, and produce the reactive behavior which provokes the high-priests of a patriarchal society to label them as hysterical, neurotic, or psychotic. The old label of "possession" is marginally less degrading than this.

From some such conditions Jesus may have released Mary of Magdala, allowing her to know herself for the first time as whole and sane, her energy and power as holy and right.

From that moment her life centered itself on his friendship, and the service to which he had called her. A number of other women shared that experience, as we have seen, but it is also apparent that the relationship between Jesus and Mary of Magdala was of a special quality. Though she was probably not identical with Mary of Bethany she certainly claimed the role of disciple, though it is hard to imagine the energetic Mary sitting at his feet in any but a formal sense, for long at a time. Mary not only claimed the status of a disciple — she was accorded it in a particular way. There was an understanding that Mary had a special relationship with Jesus, which is apparent in several references. In Matthew and Mark she appears only in the narrative of the passion and resurrection, where in each there is the little list of women who were present, and waited, and came to the tomb and saw visions of angels, or of Jesus himself. The names vary, they seem to be a selection from among those with which we have become familiar, but in each case Mary of Magdala is mentioned, and in each case her name comes first. She is the one who cannot be forgotten, the natural leader whom it is essential to mention. In Luke's reference to the women who followed and served Jesus, Mary's name is first also. But John's gospel gives us the clearest intimation of her status, for at the crucifixion the mother of Jesus is there, with her sister, but the only other woman mentioned is Mary of Magdala. She somehow sums up, for John, the other women disciples, and this is even clearer in his beautiful account of the appearance of Jesus to Mary. In Matthew, Jesus appears to several women, including the Magdalene, but in John's account Mary is alone, and her personal grief and single-minded attachment to her Master are strongly conveyed. If there were other women there, John is not interested. He focusses on this one, close and unique relationship and shows it to us in all its intimacy, tenderness and trust.

The encounter evoked by John is both mysterious and very down to earth, and in this it is typical of the sense, conveyed by all four evangelists, that experience of the risen Jesus was quite unpredictable and yet, at the time, very direct and simple, even everyday. When Mary came to the tomb she was looking for the dead, with the passionate concern of one who loves deeply, but her love was focussed on one who was certainly dead. The body was the only thing left to her, in the depths of a grief which was perhaps greater than that of any other of the followers of Jesus. Her love, like that of the other women, was much less mixed up with personal ambition and even Messianic hope. Though certainly the vision of a kingdom of freedom and peace was vivid for them, it was the liberating friendship they had known which remained the heart of their relationship with Jesus, a liberation they were learning to extend to others. For them all, but especially for Mary of Magdala, the central experience of the last terrible days was the grieving. The confusion of horror and pain, disillusion and death was over, too recent to be understood, too close to be touched. There remained the last shred of comfort, the hope of caring for the dead which has always been the women's prerogative until the hospitals and professionals took it over. But when Mary came to the place, the expected duty and comfort of that service was snatched from her. With the others, she was confronted by nothing but emptiness, a space where the body was not, therefore further loss beyond the wrenching loss already suffered. John's account tells us much about Mary, and the way in which she was different from the other women. He tells us that she ran immediately to tell her friends what she had seen, whereas the women in the synoptic accounts stayed around.

It is in this scene that Mary is shown to us as the first witness of the resurrection, the first to preach the good news, and in John's account there is no hint of the rejection of the woman's message.

Deprived of their goal in coming, the women were for a while purposeless, suspended in bewilderment, while Mary moved at once in pursuit of her goal, and called others to respond. Her report to the men was a call to action, she wanted the body recovered from the "they" who had taken it. The two men ran back with her through the still shadowy streets, galvanized by her urgency out of the lethargy of horror. They came and saw, but whatever conclusions they drew, whatever their feelings, they went back again. It is interesting that John shows us Mary, not going into the tomb with the two other disciples, not noticing what they noticed, but remaining outside. Perhaps she came behind them more slowly, having already run the same distance to fetch them, but it seems as if, unlike Peter and John, she saw no sense in going in where, she knew, the body of the Lord was not. She may even have felt some anger and impatience at the behaviour of the two men. After they had gone, she stayed where she was and cried — abandoned, wretched, and frustrated by the impossibility of doing anything positive. It was only then that she peered into the dark space, perhaps feeling that she could at least carry in her mind the image of the place.

How do we interpret the evangelist's story of what happened next — or indeed any of the resurrection stories? That all the evangelists shaped the material to emphasize their theological conclusions is undoubted. They were writing out of an already developed Christology, different in each case. They were interpreting for their particular churches issues which were vital and controversial in those communities. In doing so they drew on an existing corpus of stories, told and retold from the beginning. The earliest official proclamations of the resurrection to audiences beyond Jerusalem does not seem to have included mention of the women or the empty tomb, for reasons I have discussed earlier, yet the stories spread by the women were widely known and could not be denied. In time they became an accepted part of the preaching, hallowed by usage, essential to any sharing of the good news. The persistence of these stories, in spite of the earlier censorship, is itself evidence of their basis in verifiable personal experience. The women had told what happened to them. Their accounts varied with their personalities; one felt one emotion, another reacted differently, and their first hearers also chose one or another feature as salient. So the versions varied a little, yet the basis of them was the witness of still living and well-known women.

Mary of Magdala was among the best known, and if John gives her a central role that is because her role was indeed central, and perhaps also because she was, for a time at least, a member of the church for which he wrote, a church which, as we have seen, accorded a higher status and a larger role to women than the Jerusalem church. That his account of what happened is basically Mary's account seems reasonable to assume, and the resemblance of the story in certain features to resurrection stories in the synoptic gospels (the surprise element, the failure to recognize followed by revelation, the commissioning) also lessens the scope for the development of theological themes applied to the story rather than growing out of it. What we have is basically Mary's own experience, put into words by someone accustomed to her style of preaching and acting, but also incorporating themes common to the women's proclamation as it was known to all the churches. For instance, the apparition of a divine messenger in the tomb is mentioned, but there is no hint of awe or amazement, let alone fear, from this Mary. She is still concentrated on the one fact which preoccupies her, and therefore not open to anything further. One wonders if she really saw anything, or whether, comparing notes later with the other women, she realized that what she had been only marginally and reluctantly aware of was indeed the potent presence to which her friends, less willful and obsessed and more receptive, had been sensitive and responsive. She was not yet willing to open herself to any awareness that challenged her concentration on her grief.

The words of a stranger, who had appeared behind her, were at first no more than a repetition of the question she had already answered so dismissively. It is impossible to guess at the tone, or the emphasis of the words. Was there, in the repeated question, a demand that she ask herself more closely the reason for her ceaseless weeping? Was she clinging to her version of the predicament, not willing to see that something else was present? "What are you weeping for? Who is it you are looking for?" There are even echoes of the question put in Luke's gospel to the two gloomy disciples on the road to Emmaus — "What is it you are debating as you walk?"

The extended question challenges Mary to ask herself what she really wants — the dead, as she had decided, or the living? But she cannot let go. The tenacity which made her what she was, which was her strength, is also easily a wilful blindness, a clinging to her own preconceptions. She can only think in terms of the dead love whose body she needs to care for. "Tell me where you have laid him, and I will take him away," for she has to be in control, able to cope, even in the midst of loss and tragedy.

The way through that self-absorbed blindness was to recall her to the relationship which had once saved her from the prison of a self-contained world of delusion and fear. He called her by name, called her out as he had done before: "Mary". And at that she came out of her obsessive misery as she had done once before, without hesitation and completely, dropping the whole wretched mess as if she dropped an ugly garment and forgot it. She hailed him and reached out to him, claiming him, as before she had claimed grief for him. He had to re-direct the force of her passionate joy, and the theology of this very explicit re-direction of energy is profound. In the response of Jesus, John shows us forcibly the presence of the risen Lord as being primarily in the little ones, the community of the loved and the needy. "Go to my brothers —" and share with them the awareness that the whole relationship has changed, that their love is caught up into a completeness they could not have imagined. John underlines it, in a phrase deliberately contrasting the old with the new. This God with whom Mary, and all the others, are in process of being incorporated is not only "my Father", and "my God", but now equally "your Father" and "your God". Mary's outpouring of love is not refused but transformed, it is to her a means of creating the new community of the little ones. "I have seen the Lord", she told them, and she told them all that had happened.

The church for which John's gospel was written was clearly accustomed to women as preachers and teachers, as we saw in connection with the story of the Samaritan woman. In the resurrection story Mary's role as confidant of the Lord and privileged messenger is very clear, and it is also preserved for us in the apocryphal gospels. Mary Magdalene appears as the leader of the "holy women" in the book called "Sophia Jesu Christi", though all the women are equally disciples with the men. In the *Pistis Sophia*, of the third century, which consists mostly of questions addressed to Jesus on "secret" doctrine and answered by him, thirty-nine out of the forty-six questions are placed in the mouth of Mary Magdalene; Mary and John are the two especially privileged and enlightened ones. In several of these books Mary leads not only the women but the men; it is she who encourages and exhorts the men when they are faint-hearted. In the *Gospel of Mary*, when Mary's leadership and prominence is challenged by other disciples, Levi answers the critics in strong words: "If the Saviour has made her worthy, who then art thou to reject her? Certainly the Saviour knew her surely enough. Therefore he did love her more than us." This text is primarily the reflection of the struggle of gnostic and other heretical churches to maintain and justify the leadership of women in their congregations, but the interest of these and similar passages in the present context is that when the writer wanted a woman who would most fitly embody the women's role, which he (or she?) was justifying, it was Mary Magdalene who naturally came to mind.

These "gospels" date from the second and third centuries — some possibly from very late in the first century, in the light of the tendency of recent scholars to push the dating of the canonical gospels back to earlier dates, mostly before 70 A.D. It is always a mistake to dismiss documents as historically valueless simply because their obvious and primary purpose is polemic and doctrinal. There may well be traces in these writings of authentic teachings of Jesus, though couched in the esoteric language of gnostic doctrine. Certainly the writers believed that they were conveying authentic tradition in their own way, and the names of the apostles are used in the dialogues to lend authority to the teaching. It is significant, therefore, that Mary Magdelene is so prominent, though other women play leading roles also. Her reputation carries conviction, her name is that of a known and revered teacher and preacher, on equal terms with the Twelve and often mentioned as superior to them in intimacy with the Lord.

The oddity of Mary's disappearance from the early Christian scene (along with all the other women) as recorded in "Acts" has been discussed earlier, and some of the reasons suggested. The prominence of Mary Magdalene in the passion and resurrection narratives in all four gospels only underlines the strangeness of her absence afterwards, and the gnostic gospels, plus some historical reconstruction, suggest a very good reason for it. Raymond Brown, among others, has shown how the Jerusalem church, and others founded directly from it, were in tension with the churches founded by Paul. (The Roman Church was a Jerusalem foundation; this explains Paul's careful explanation and justification of his doctrine when addressing the church in Rome). The Jerusalem church clung vigorously to a modified synagogue form of organization. Though it preached the risen Lord and Saviour it was still markedly Jewish in cultural attitudes. It was critical of deviations from the Jewish norm, as we can see from the reaction of the Elders there to Peter's acceptance of Gentile converts (as exemplified by Cornelius) on equal terms with those of Jewish origin. They were able to accept this and other big changes because they were men of faith and courage, but unless specifically challenged they tended to remain — not unnaturally —

attached to familiar ways. And no cultural conditioning is stronger than that which determines sex roles. There was, as I have suggested, quite a severe struggle around this issue. It is never mentioned, but the conclusion seems unavoidable that there was a confrontation over the roles of women at quite an early stage in the development of the Jerusalem-centered church. This may be the reason for the emphasis on the role of women in the gospel of John, representing a church whose tradition diverged in some ways from that of the Jerusalem tradition, and indeed in other respects from the Pauline churches as well.

Whatever happened in the Johannine churches, the Jerusalem church seems to have suffered something like a purge. This involved a number of women, but it probably also concerned the roles of members of Jesus' family, especially his mother. I shall be writing more about her later, but her position in the church was a center of the controversy around Jesus' relatives and around the women. If there was a movement to prevent "the family" from taking over the church, the focus of this was probably Mary, mother of Jesus, not only his closest relative but a woman of strong vision and personality. Dealing with her, however, meant dealing with the other women who, for all their differences, formed a strong group. Jesus had given these women unprecedented freedom, and the men in the church could not live with this. Their whole cultural identity was threatened by the behaviour of the women, and in the end the sheer weight of custom was stronger than the impulse of new life. The memories of the life, death and resurrection of Jesus were too clear, the stories already too widely known and established, to be contradicted, so these women do appear in the gospels. But in Acts there is no trace of them once the day of Pentecost was over. Along with Mary, mother of Jesus, they are there, they are empowered by the Holy Spirit, and then, apparently, they evaporate. But Luke's silence, dictated by the only versions of earlier events available to him, does not reflect the whole Christian experience. The importance of women in the spread of the gospel in the Gentile world we shall see in the next chapter, as well as the fact that within a few decades stories about Mary Magdalene were finally embedded in the tradition of gnostic and other groups which were marginal to the mainstream church. (We have to remember, in using words like "heretical" and "mainstream" who it was who so defined them. "Heretical" groups are always the ones who failed to win. History is written by the victors.)

Mary's role in the gnostic gospels is that of one who teaches and preaches — the complaint against her by Peter at one point is that she "never stops talking", which really means that the men can no longer do all the talking. But these gospels are not narrative, they are doctrine in dialogue form, and tell us nothing about events. They give no hint about where Mary was or what she was doing, after Pentecost. Later legends fill the gap. A whole series of legends makes her a missionary to France — that is, Gaul. She and Martha and Lazarus, and assorted others, are said to have escaped persecution in Palestine and drifted on a rudderless boat to Marseilles, where they settled and began to preach and evangelize.

The rudderless craft is a very suitable symbol of the precarious nature of the women's journey, away from all that was familiar, towards an unknown land, with nothing but unprecedented faith and courage to guide them. But there is nothing at all improbable in the tradition that these women were among a group which decided to leave behind a situation where their message was unheard and their service rejected, and to take the good news to a well-known and populous Roman port, the gateway to lands to which no other messengers had yet penetrated. It would be natural for these women to choose not to join in the work initiated by Paul and his colleagues. The early missionaries tried not to duplicate each other's efforts in any case, and it is possible that Paul's controversial doctrine and style, as reported in the talk of the other churches, might make it seem desirable to branch out independently, as indeed the Johannine church had done. Though it seems possible that Mary and others actually formed part of that church for a time, or perhaps of some other group at a distance from Jerusalem, they were, by nature and by commissioning, missionaries, and the decision to travel is not at all unlikely or out of character.

All this is speculation, but it is essential to speculate; this spinning of possibilities is the only way to break the spell of silence which has distorted the role of women as persons and as Christians. If we can *imagine* women like Mary and Martha planning and carrying out a mission to Marseilles, and then realize that such a development fits the few indications we have of their character, and their relationship with Jesus, then we have done much to get free from the paralyzing effects of official church history. Historians are no longer contemptuous of folk memory, they admit the accuracy and insight to be found in "legends". It is unlikely that we can ever establish with certainty that such a wild bunch of missionaries landed in the harbours of Gaul, but then we can never establish with certainty the truth of many of the things Christians believe. What is important is to be free to perceive the effect Jesus had on these women and to take courage and hope from them. What is certain is that areas of southern France have been the home of stories about Martha and Mary and their companions for two thousand years.

If Mary Magdalene is the representative of the other empowered women in the dialogues of the gnostic gospels, Martha outdistanced her in medieval legend. Martha became the representative of women seeking a role of active service and caring, reaching beyond the cloister and into the streets. (This was after the women's monasteries had ceased to be islands of sanity, culture, healing and hospitality in a barbaric world, and had become cloistered prisons for dangerous females.)

Martha, in one legend, tamed a dangerous dragon and led it away tied to her girdle like a puppy. But the rather sickening end to this story tells how the people of the town, who had been so afraid of the dragon, then took courage and killed the tamed dragon with stones and spears. The symbolism is revealing and depressing. St. George's method of dealing with dragons is obviously preferable in the mind of a male-dominated culture and church. It is much easier to kill or suppress, easier to put violent people in prison than heal the sources of violence, easier to assault disease with surgery and drugs than to educate towards wholeness of body and mind. Martha stands for the women and men who overcome evil by the acuteness of their insight and compassion, and Martha's iconography, in medieval paintings and statues, indicates an image of her as heroic, strong and firm. She is not young but matronly, a handsome woman, capable and comforting like the best kind of maiden aunt.

In fact, Martha may well have been a widow. She is clearly designated as head of her household and of her family at Bethany. When the two sisters and brother are mentioned Martha's name usually comes first. Some have speculated that "Simon the Leper" was the deceased husband or father of Martha. Martha, in any case, headed her household, and the most likely reason is that she was a widow or else the eldest daughter, caring for a younger brother and sister after their father's death, and recognizably the one in charge though her brother might be legal owner of the property.

Martha was different from many of the women we encounter in the gospels in that most of them left their homes and normal surroundings in order to follow Jesus; for many people whose lives are radically changed, the change often requires a change of place. In their case this was often really necessary because of likely persecution from outraged families, but also because the pressure of habitual expectations and patterns of behaviour easily become too strong for the newly liberated woman whose new self-image is still fragile. But Martha remained in her own home, and this fact alone gives us an idea of her personality. She was a person who was in charge of her own life, who knew her strength and gifts and could use them. Because of her freedom from parental or conjugal pressures she had a self-confidence that many other women lacked, but it was narrow. Like so many before and after her, she created a satisfying role within the limits assigned to her, and because she found it adequate she was not much inclined to question the limits. The management of a large and hospitable household was a taxing task requiring a good head for business, an ability to direct and organize people, and much skill in the arts of the garden, kitchen and still-room, besides spinning, weaving, the preparation of remedies and care of the sick. She had to know how to do all these things but also how to train others to do them, and oversee their work. (It is no wonder that the demand for a wider *public* role for women came at a period when women of the upper classes were relieved of such outlets for energy and talent by social pressures, and became thoroughly bored in consequence.)

This was the woman to whose home Jesus was introduced, perhaps by a friend or relative. It may be, even, that the friendship was an old one, and that the Bethany family had been friends of Jesus' own family, a place where from boyhood he had been accustomed to visit on the yearly pilgrimages to Jerusalem. In any case he was welcome and comfortable there, and in time his followers also were received there. In this we can get an idea of Martha's quality as a person. She was able to allow people to grow. When the young Galilean began to attract attention, and disciples, and also adverse criticism, she was not afraid of the neighbors' opinions, and continued to make her home available to the group. They would gather there, and others too would come in and listen and talk. She provided beds and food, and that atmosphere of leisure which enables people to relax and encounter each other in the most favourable way.

It seems likely that in the famous Martha and Mary story we do catch a glimpse of what might be called Martha's conversion. Her affection for Jesus, and in time her growing respect for him as a man of deep spirituality, a teacher and healer, demanded no more of her than what a habitually generous and loving woman could easily compass. She would love him, and serve him, without in any way moving outside the normal categories of her way of life. Perhaps she didn't take in very much of what was said in the gatherings in her home. She would take time, when she was not too busy, to join the group and listen to the parables Jesus told, and his answers to questions, but although some of it stirred her oddly, it was all in the tradition of her faith, and she could listen and ponder and be grateful.

What may have seemed questionable to her was the addition of women to the group which frequented her home. Their absence from their own homes was disturbing, yet Jesus had healed them and called them, he must have his reasons. She welcomed them also, and it may be that in listening to them, asking them the questions that women ask each other, she began to perceive a strange and very disturbing element in the teaching of the young Rabbi she had befriended and cared for, one which did not fit her assumptions about the relations between the sexes or the role of women. Yet some of these had been very sick or abused women. That made a difference. It was when her own sister, neither sick nor abused, behaved so oddly that Martha had to face personally the implications of an acceptance of Jesus as friend. Members of a family, even very affectionate ones, may often live closely together, and care for each other, yet not easily talk about experiences which disturb or absorb them. It may have come as a complete shock to Martha to realize that her sister had somehow come to perceive herself as a disciple of the Rabbi. Her first reaction, seeing her sister sitting there with the others, was to feel that Mary didn't understand what she was doing, had been moved by Jesus' teaching, which was good and right, and had been influenced by the other women who were, for whatever reason, outside their normal environment. She had allowed herself unthinkingly to lose touch with her own proper role, the role in which Martha had trained her, lovingly and fully. And Jesus, man-like, had not realized the results of allowing that to happen.

Martha was disturbed, and showed it, but she felt that it would be enough to point out to Jesus the situation he had allowed to develop. The shock came when he made it clear that he was fully aware of what

Mary was doing and of the implications of her behaviour and that he approved. He was challenging Martha to recognize a demand that over-rode the demands of her woman's world. She was forced, there in her own little kingdom, to recognize a power that could break down the defenses of that kingdom and call her to move beyond them, to be vulnerable, not in control, drifting on a raft driven by the unpredictable wind of the Spirit.

What went on in the mind of Martha in the weeks and months that followed we can only guess. What we know is that at a certain point, not too long after, it was Martha who was able to formulate the great confession of faith: "You are the Christ."

The passage in John's gospel (11:17-44) is among the most famous in the New Testament, but the focus is usually on what happened to Lazarus. The conversation with Martha has been played down, and most people seem quite unaware that in it Martha makes the great proclamation which the synoptics put into Peter's mouth. Peter's claim to a unique position in the church has been justified by commentators in terms of his insight in making that confession. No such special role has been ascribed to Martha, yet in John's version her words are fuller and more explicit than Peter's. This is one of four encounters between Jesus and a woman in John's gospel, all of which are full of paradox and theologically charged. The encounter with the woman of Samaria, and with Mary of Magdala in the garden, we have already touched on, and that with the mother of Jesus will be relevant in another chapter. The one with Martha is arguably the most important, and contains the clearest Christological statement, apart from Thomas' confession after the resurrection — "My Lord and my God."

Martha's reaction to Jesus' tardy return to Bethany had been a mixture of reproach, affection and questioning. "If you had been here my brother would not have died." John ascribes to Martha a more matter-of-fact statement than the demanding tone of Mary in her later meeting with Jesus. Martha states a fact, a fact she does not understand. Jesus could have saved his friend, yet he did not. "Even now" he can act with the power of God. She is feeling for a statement that she cannot allow her imagination to compass. Jesus prompts her, leading her into new regions, yet by known ways, for she believes already, with many of her people, in the final resurrection. "Your brother will rise again ..."

"Yes, I know he will rise again, at the resurrection on the last day ..."

"But ... I *am* the resurrection — do you believe that?"

When he asked her she found she did indeed know. Whatever form the conversation took which John shaped to such a strong theological point, it seemed to him to be a crucial one. John knew Martha well, if he was indeed John-bar-Zebedee, and if not, then "John" knew the experience of Zebedee's son very well indeed. He was almost certainly present when this conversation took place, and so were others who could correct him if he distorted it. It is unlikely we have a verbatim record, but, unlike the other stories of encounters with women in John, we are dealing with a very public conversation; if John says that Martha said what he makes her say, then she probably did. What she said was, "I now believe that you are the Messiah, the Son of God who was to come into the world."

What exactly Martha meant by those words, or what her hearers took her to mean, or what the evangelist meant his hearers to understand her to mean, are different things. Those phrases have accumulated so much theological baggage through the centuries that it is now virtually impossible to get behind all that and to touch into the sense they might have had when first spoken. But, whatever may have been their exact resonance and weight in the mind of that Jewish housewife, they were certainly a turning point. This was one of those moments when Jesus led people to surpass what they had thought themselves capable of, and so to discover a new self, in a new world. When her brother emerged from the grave, Martha emerged also from the very comfortable prison of her own competence and benevolent power.

But the power and competence remained. They always do. We hear no more in the gospels or "Acts" about Martha, but it seems unsurprising that such a woman proved difficult to push back into the mould from which she had broken free.

If we place side by side these two women — Martha, and her very different friend, Mary of Magdala — and realize that although outstanding they were not unique, that there were many women with them, full of intelligence, energy, talent, experience and wisdom, all convinced of their empowerment by the risen Lord, then we have little difficulty in understanding the reaction of the Jerusalem elders, or the legends that show us these women in distant lands, preaching and teaching, healing and liberating. It would take more than a dragon to intimidate such disciples.

The early crisis over the role of women was not the last. The evidence of the later epistles makes clear that the suppression of the women, their relegation to subsidiary roles and submissive attitudes, was a long and difficult struggle requiring much argument and denunciation, appeals to dubious Scriptural warrants or, if that proved to be inadequate, the exercise of sheer patriarchal fiat. A society, Jewish or Gentile, to which male dominance was so intrinsic that it was as unnoticed as the salt in daily bread simply could not adjust to the notion of women as full equals. It was as if a great tide of glory and new vision had washed over the people Jesus called, and who were driven out to call others. In the strange and transforming light of that washed world each person was new, sparkling, glorious. But the tide ebbed, people had to engage in common pursuits of that world, and the converted looked at each other in the light they shared with others whom the cleansing tide had not reached. In that common light men saw women no longer as companions, lovers and friends but as what they had always been — servants, prostitutes, breeders. When those women persisted in behaving like people newborn the results were predictable.

It seems fairly certain that many of the women were quite content to return to their familiar roles, which indeed most had never left. They were conditioned to them as much as the men, and adjusted fairly well, as enslaved people generally do. The resistance was not total, or it could not have been crushed. It was significant, however. We have one strong indication of the way things went in the fact that a number of heretical sects were led by women as well as men, and gave equal status to both. We have to remind ourselves once more that history is written by the victor. The description of one group as "orthodox" and others as "heretical" is naturally assigned by those who regard themselves as orthodox, but historically the labels stick when the self-defined orthodox are the winners; in other words the orthodox are those whose prestige and influence have given them the power to suppress any challenge. But it is significant that those Church Fathers who denounced the "heretical" sects often chose the sects' exaltation of women as a strong proof of their evil and error. Indeed in some cases this seems to have been the only reason that could be found for condemning them. The Montanists, for instance, were doctrinally in line with at least one stream of contemporary orthodoxy, but their leaders along with Montanus were two women prophets, Priscilla and Maximilla. They claimed no more than was claimed for male prophets in the early days (the stage crystallized by the *Didache*), but they were women, and the patriarchal churches reacted with revulsion and condemnation.

We get the impression, then, that groups in which the equal role and leadership of women was well-established and working harmoniously tended to separate themselves from churches in which the patriarchal reaction was strong. There was at this time in the first and second centuries no *one* centralized form of doctrine and practice, but many variants, constantly argued, and condemning each other. Those who did not agree naturally drew apart. But the churches within which a patriarchal tendency was reasserting itself were more acceptable to the "outside" world (which was one reason Paul gave for requiring conformity by women to the sexual norms of society in general) and also less threatening to each other. So the dominant patriarchal churches rapidly acquired more and more unity, and also more and more social acceptability. In times of persecution the sexual roles dissolved, as we shall see in the story of Perpetua and Felicity, but when the faithful could return to "normal" life the sexual norms of the secular world reasserted themselves.

This pattern has continued through the centuries. Groups which have rediscovered the original spirit and freedom and power of the gospel have also rediscovered the equal leadership of women. Some have withdrawn from the patriarchal church, some have been forced out. Some women managed to establish small enclaves of feminine autonomy and liberty within the patriarchal structure, as in the case of early monastic women, and some missionary societies of Protestant women in the nineteenth century. These organizations have for the most part been gradually modified or squeezed into shape by one of the strongest emotional forces in any society, the male fear of the female. Jesus was not afraid of women, and as a result a whole edifice of myth, prejudice and rationalization was shattered, but even his influence, in this *one* area, could not endure. Almost anything he taught could be accepted — even, for short periods, detachment from material prosperity — but the equal freedom of men and women as children of God was too difficult. The more we consider it, the less surprising it seems that even those courageous and dedicated men who had given up so much to follow the Master found themselves unable to tolerate what they felt to be the unnatural and arrogant behaviour of women like Martha, and Mary of Magdala.

On the other hand, there is the fact, attested grudgingly by Luke and very clearly by Paul, that the role of women in the early missionary churches was different. There, the relationship which Jesus had with Mary and Martha and others seems to have subsisted for a while between men and women missionaries, among whom the women were not servants, but friends.

VII. FELLOW WORKERS FOR CHRIST

Lydia was the owner of a purple dye business in Philippi, an important city of Macedonia, which was a Roman province. She was a business woman, and perhaps by way of business had moved from her home town of Thyatira in Lydia. ("Lydia" was probably her surname, and pinpoints her origin just as people nowadays are sometimes called "Hill" or "England".)

Lydia was a Greek, but like many "pagans" at a time when the religion of Rome was decadent, she was searching for something more meaningful and real than the merely formal and political religions of the Empire, or the residual local and rural versions of Greek worship. Like the Centurion, Cornelius, and many others, Lydia had come in contact with Judaism and was attracted by its vision of a universal, transcendant God, and by the tenacious courage and fidelity of its people. She was not a "proselyte" (a foreign convert to Judaism) but she "revered God," which meant she joined in worship, and listened to Scripture. Paul, Silas and Luke came to Philippi on Paul's second missionary journey, as a result of a dream, so Luke tells us, in which he had seen a Macedonian appealing to him, "Come over to Macedonia". At this stage Paul, (like Jesus in his own early ministry) made a habit of going first to the synagogue in each place, but in Philippi, it seems, they did not find one.

Perhaps the local Jewish community was too small and poor to afford a synagogue, or perhaps the one they had was too small for growing numbers, but the warm weather made outdoor worship possible and pleasant, at a place by the river which afforded quiet and privacy. This was important for Lydia, for in a normal synagogue women would be segregated behind a curtain or grille, or perhaps upstairs, whereas in the open they could see and be seen, even though they sat separately. Perhaps, even, this unusual place of prayer accounts for the fact that a pagan woman had access to Jewish teaching and worship at all. It certainly accounts for the fact that she saw and heard Paul when he attended the service and spoke. But he took the further step of approaching the women he saw there and talking to them particularly. Perhaps the women asked him to; perhaps he saw in them that hunger and hope which told him that God had been before him. It may have been Lydia herself who took the initiative in approaching him. In any case she opened her heart in response to what he said. She was so moved by his proclamation of the gospel that she professed her faith and demanded baptism.

Luke condenses the whole affair into two sentences, and perhaps indeed events were as rapid as he seem to suggest. Not only Lydia, but "all her household" were baptized. Her household in this case would mean not merely her family but her employees, apprentices and servants, but this is nothing like the later mass baptisms of subjects and servants at the order of convert kings in Gaul and Britain, when the candidate had no choice. If Lydia's household came to baptism in a body it must have been because her enthusiasm impressed them, but also because they themselves were impressed by the preaching. Some, perhaps, were worshipping with her that morning in the open air place of prayer, and shared the experience of Paul's preaching. There are curious echoes of the story of the Samaritan woman, running home to tell all the village about the wonderful man she had met. It seems possible, from Luke's way of putting it, that in fact Lydia did hurry back to her house, which was clearly not far away, and summon her household to come and see for themselves, there and then. In the leisurely Sabbath atmosphere Paul and his friends might well have stopped for several hours to preach, to answer questions, to develop budding faith and to baptize, and we can imagine Lydia imperiously summoning everyone to hurry out and to hear for themselves. Evidently she was a loved, respected, and strong-minded woman, but it was the teaching itself which convinced them all.

They were baptized — but that was only the beginning, and the hunger for truth which had driven Lydia to listen to Paul was sharpened rather than satiated. She felt, as many do, that she had just begun to live and to learn. There was so much to discover! She wasted no time. "If you have judged me to be a believer in the Lord, I beg you to come and stay in my house", she said, making it hard for Paul to make an excuse — for if he refused it would seem to imply a lack of trust in those he had just baptized. "She insisted on our going," Luke adds, summing up an argument in which Lydia, the business woman, got her own way in a deal.

That phrase of Luke's sums up a lot. "She insisted", she did not give up — in some translations, "She would not take 'no' for an answer." That was what women had to do, and did, in the early days of the movement created by the Resurrection of Jesus. They had to insist, because although the attitude of Jesus had been so clear and although, in fidelity to him, some at least of his followers accepted the amazing revolution in sexual roles and customs, to do so went clean against the traditional mind-set of both Jewish and Gentile converts to faith in Jesus. Those men and women who claimed for women an equal role in the proclamation of the gospel and in all that went with it were swimming against the cultural stream. They had to "insist".

Lydia's insistence succeeded. Not only did Paul and Silas and Luke stay at her home on that occasion but that action established a pattern. Lydia was, no doubt, already a leader, the owner of a successful business, carrying weight as a person of consequence in the community. In the Roman world, women who were not of the middle class had more legal rights and more social freedom than Jewish women. Wealthy women, poor women, and women in trades and businesses were free of at least some of the restrictions imposed on middle-class wives. It was natural for Lydia's large house to be a gathering place, and it became the center for new believers in that area, for Lydia did not rest with the conversion of her own household. She passed the word around, and many people, friends and neighbors, shopkeepers and merchants, came to listen to Lydia's remarkable guests, to ask questions, to discern, to pray, and in many cases to be baptized also. Lydia's house became a house-church, a center for worship and instruction, but also, — in obedience to the teaching of Jesus — a center of hospitality and care for any in need. In a very short time "Lydia's place" was the obvious place for believers to go.

Not long after, it seems, Paul and Silas were imprisoned and flogged on the accusation of citizens who feared their strange power, and were released in an even stranger way. The amazed and frightened jailer was converted by the experience, and he and his household were baptized that very night, after which he washed their wounds and gave them a good meal! But it is interesting that when, later, the city authorities persuaded their disconcerting visitors to leave, the missionaries did not do so until they had been back to Lydia's home to meet "their fellow Christians" and tell them all about it, and speak words of encouragement.

We hear no more of Lydia, but we know enough. She was one of those leaders of the early days who established and developed strong, small communities of the new faith, based in their homes. And a great many of the members were women.

We saw earlier that households in which Jesus habitually stayed during his ministry naturally became gathering places for those whose lives he had touched. They came there to be with him, but they continued to come there afterward to share what was happening to them and to support each other. This must have happened in many other homes, too, where believers told others and formed new groups which became the basis of local churches after the preaching of the Resurrection began. We are shown glimpses of a few of them — a group in Samaria, many households in Jerusalem. In much more detail we learn of the formation of one of the first Gentile house-churches in the home of Cornelius. The house in Capharnaum which belonged to Simon Peter and where Jesus made his home for a while is certainly known, from archeological evidence, to have been a place of meeting and worship in the very early days of Christianity. We can safely assume a continuity between the time when Jesus stayed there himself and the time when his followers scratched Christian signs in the stonework. And we can tell who was in charge of that household. It was "Peter's wife's mother" to whom Jesus was summoned in a hurry to heal her fever, for presumably the whole household ground to a halt when her controlling hand was withdrawn. So, later, when Peter's wife went off with her husband on missionary journeys (so Paul says, anyway) her mother was presumably the one who continued to make that home a place where the teaching of Jesus was expounded and his constant presence asserted and celebrated.

The home in Bethany was clearly another such center, as we have seen, but how it developed later can only be a matter of speculation. We do, however, have one example of an early house-church led by a woman. It spans the period from the ministry of Jesus to the early development of the church, and that is the home of Mary, mother of John Mark. She is referred to in passing by Luke (Acts 12:12-17) because it was to her home that Peter went after he had been mysteriously released from prison. "A large company was at prayer" in the house, so evidently it was a sizable house, with a courtyard and an outer door on which Peter knocked until the servant girl, Rhoda, came to see who was making such a noise. It is a very believable tale, of a girl so excited she rushed back in with the news instead of opening the gate, leaving poor Peter still banging away. The others thought it must be a ghost, but at her insistence they finally opened up, making such a din that Peter couldn't make himself heard. All this points to a large gathering and a habitual one. This was not, however, the headquarters of the Jerusalem church, for Peter had to send a message to "James and the members of the Church" about what had happened. This is an odd phrase, at least superficially implying that those around James were members of the Church in a sense in which those assembled in Mary's home were not, and it seems likely, in fact, that the church in Mary's home consisted of Hellenists — Greek-speaking Jews who had settled in the area. (Rhoda is a Greek name.) We know there was friction, or at least distance between the Hellenists and the Judean Jews. Mary's son, John Mark, travelled with Paul and Barnabas, who was his cousin, or possibly his uncle, and later there was a temporary split between Mark and Paul. The internal politics of the infant church were already quite complicated. But there is no doubt that Mark's mother, Mary, presided over a large gathering of believers and that this was a usual place for Peter to go, since his voice was very familiar to the servants. This may be an indication that the Hellenists, less attached to the religious establishment of Jerusalem than James and his group, found it easier to accept the leadership of women. It seems clear that the role of women in the Hellenist gatherings was indeed one of the sources of tension between the two factions, for Luke tells us in *Acts* that the Hellenists complained that their widows were overlooked in the daily distribution. This may well mean that the leading Jewish apostles refused to allow these women to share in the breaking of bread, perhaps because of unorthodox behaviour. But Luke's account of Peter in other places shows him more open to Gentiles than James' party, and this fits the story of his going first to Mary's home. We are evidently in touch with hints of a very stormy situation, with the role of women at the heart of the storm, as I suggested in the last chapter.

Then there was Dorcas, or Tabitha. Her two names, Greek and Hebrew, indicate the way in which her hometown of Joppa on the Mediterranean brought the Jews there in close contact and interaction with the Greek culture spread and sustained by the constant traffic by sea. She was a woman of great vigour and generosity, one whom the local community mourned when she died, but especially the poor. The news of her restoration to life "spread all over Joppa", and even allowing for a typical Lukean exaggeration we are evidently hearing about a person whose life and work was central to the community. The traditional image of Dorcas as a homebody who liked to sew (and gave her name to groups of churchwomen who make garments for the poor) is a typical distortion. Evidently her talents included dressmaking, but if that had been her only contribution her death would hardly have excited such distress and dismay.

Many times we have to make do with hints only, yet the hints are many. Paul chose a young Christian called Timothy to travel with him, (*Acts* 16:1-4) and had the youth circumcised "out of consideration for the Jews who lived in those parts, who all knew that his father was a Gentile." (This is one of those disturbingly typical instances where Paul, who "denounced Peter to his face" for refusing to eat with Gentiles for fear of the Jews, himself compromised his own loudly stated principles.) Timothy's mother was a Jewish-Christian called Eunice, and his grandmother was called Lois. Paul refers to them affectionately as "his mother and mine". They were people who had cared for him and in whose home he had taught, as he did in Lydia's.

Evodia and Syntyche had "laboured with him in the gospel", and their role in the local church was so significant that dissension between them threatened the whole assembly. The phrase "labored with" implies something very different from mere supporter. They were co-workers, women responsible for the running of the local church.

There are so many names that it becomes dull reading, since we often know little more than the names. Tryphoena and Tryphosa who "toiled in the Lord's service" are named together in the famous sixteenth chapter of Paul's *Letter to the Romans* which is all messages, and is most probably not a part of the letter to the Romans, but of a separate one, perhaps a letter of recommendation given to Phoebe, and including messages to Christians in the church she was to visit, possibly Ephesus. Among the people mentioned is another Mary who "toiled hard," and also the controversial Junias (or Julia or Julias) whom some commentators have been anxious to make into a man, but the name is almost certainly that of a woman. The reason for the desire to make her male is that Paul refers to her and her brother (or husband) not only as "fellow countrymen and comrades in captivity" but as "eminent among the *apostles*". No wonder it would be more convenient if Junias were male. In the same letter he greets "dear Persis" who has "toiled in (the Lord's) service so long". The phrase is one Paul applied to himself and some male missionaries. It does not merely mean that they worked hard; it refers to the work of preaching. These were missionaries and church leaders. There are several other women in the list, some coupled with a man's name, presumably married couples, as well as "Nereus and his sister". All these women were evidently active in ministry, and some were also leaders of house-churches, either alone or with their husbands.

Phoebe, who "holds office in the congregation at Cenchreae" was the woman for whom the letter in which these names and messages occur was probably written. Her office is often translated as that of "deaconess", but the Greek word simply indicates one who "served" the church in some capacity. The Greek word meant primarily one who served at *table*, hence the application of this term to the servers who were chosen to help in the distribution of food (or Eucharist?) in the Jerusalem congregation (*Acts* 6:1-6). The title may also refer, therefore, to those who serve at the "Lord's table", assisting at the celebration of the Eucharist, but it is doubtful if at this early stage the roles around celebration of the Supper of the Lord were particularly well-defined. It seems that the person who presided was probably either the person who presided over the house-church itself, or a visiting apostle, and since women undoubtedly functioned in both these capacities, it is considerably more likely than not that women presided at the "breaking of bread". There can be no complete proof; all we can do is to try to evoke a sense of the quality of life in these early communities, the style of relationships, the method of organization.

There is plenty of material for such an evocation, and the result is a composite picture in which women undoubtedly filled leadership roles alongside the men. The early equality began to break down quite soon, but at least for a while there was this remarkable experiment with a different social model. In it the baptismal declaration of equality in the kingdom ("neither Jew nor Gentile, neither slave nor free, neither male nor female, but all one in Jesus Christ") was actually lived out in daily life, in worship and in organization. As I have suggested, this may well have been easier, at least for a while, in the churches established in Gentile cities. Women in the later Roman society—or at least some women—had more independence, and it was not unknown for women to be magistrates, to sit on governing bodies, to run businesses or administer estates. Even the Jewish women of communities in the Diaspora had more freedom and power. But a deeper reason for the difference was probably the fact that these new churches were psychologically as well as geographically distant from Jerusalem. As we saw, the Hellenists in Jerusalem were in any case more open to different ways, if only as a way of showing that they would not be totally ruled by the Jerusalem elders of James' party. But in the great cosmopolitan, pluralist cities of the Empire the new doctrine and new life was not under immediate pressure to conform to the norms of the Jerusalem church. The new churches did not inherit the mind-set of the male Jews who dominated the original group. They soon developed their own, but for a while the radically different social model created by Jesus was able to flourish in obedience to the spirit, illuminating the teachings of Jesus himself as they were transmitted from group to group. There was variety in the ways the different churches responded, variety in the personalities that led them. There was freedom to try new things, to be different.

The story of Lydia gave us a picture of how a new church came into being, called and led by a woman from the beginning. Phoebe shows us a similar person being sent on an important mission from one church to another, and finally a couple, Priscilla and Aquila, put us in touch with the way young churches lived. These two had been part of the Jewish community living in Rome. There was much friction between Jews and the Jewish-Christians, and about A.D. 47 the Emperor Claudius expelled all the Jews, which included the Christian Jews, on the grounds that their dissension caused public disturbances. This was possibly true but could have been an excuse to get rid of the Jews who were, as always, convenient scapegoats. In any case Priscilla and Aquila went to Corinth, where Paul met them on his second missionary journey. They were tentmakers by trade, which was also Paul's trade, so it was natural for him to stay with them and help to support himself in this way, as was his custom in order to avoid being a financial burden.

It has been assumed that Paul converted Priscilla and Aquila, but research (by Raymond Brown in particular) strongly suggests that there were a large number of Christians in Rome before the expulsion under Claudius. We have to remember that *Acts* is written almost entirely about *Paul's* missionary work, after the account of the very early years in which Peter is the hero. But Paul was not the only, nor necessarily the most important, missionary to travel so widely, and it seems very likely that the Roman church was founded by missionaries coming directly from Jerusalem, possibly including Peter himself. There was probably a Christian church in Rome in the early 40's, but it was not a *Pauline* church, and its Jewishness was marked, as was that of the Jerusalem elders from whom it drew its doctrine. But this early presence of a Christian church in Rome suggests that Priscilla and Aquila were already Christians when they moved to Corinth, and when Paul arrived he found a Christian community already in existence, centered in their home. Paul used their home as his base while he was there, and evidently a deep friendship developed, for when he left there they went with him to Syria, leaving behind a well-established young church. They went to Ephesus and worked closely with Paul, and it was from there that Paul included them in the greetings he sent with his letter to Corinth. Later, Priscilla and Aquila evidently decided there was more work for them to do there, and they stayed on for a while, though Paul went off to visit churches which his earlier labors had called into being.

It seems clear that Priscilla and Aquila were a couple with a strong missionary vocation. Their work was to build up new churches, but when the new growth was established they had the freedom to let go of that and move on. They were accepted as leaders and teachers. Apollos was a follower of John the Baptist in a group which had come to faith in Jesus but had been baptized by John. He was preaching Jesus in the synagogue in Ephesus, where Priscilla and Aquila heard him, and invited him home. They "took him in hand" and instructed him more fully, presumably in the more developed Christology of Paul. Later he was sent on mission to Achaia by the Ephesian church. This is an example of the kind of thing which was expected of church leaders such as Priscilla and Aquila. The strong probability that this couple had in fact established at least a small gathering of Christians before the coming of Paul suggests a pattern in keeping with my earlier suggestion that the spreading of the gospel did not wait for those Luke regards as the official preachers, but proliferated informally. Groups of differing origin with differing interpretations of Jesus, were many. Apollos was not exceptional. Believers travelled around on business trips, or in search of employment, or for political reasons, like Priscilla and Aquila and took their faith with them. These two appear to have returned to Corinth at some point; perhaps later they went back to Rome. Their information about the church in Rome must certainly have been valuable to Paul when he was composing his great letter to that church. His love for them is evident in his greetings to them from wherever he happened to be, and his inclusion of them in his greetings to others. Priscilla's name comes first, except in one instance. This marriage was an equal partnership of two gifted and dedicated people on whom lay the responsibility for the care and upbuilding of more than one new church. (It is an indication of the sexist assumption of biblical commentators that in several biblical dictionaries, commentaries and encyclopedias, if one looks for the name Priscilla, the instruction is "see Aquila".)

It is this routine assumption, from that day to this, of the unimportance of women's role in the apostolic church which makes it hard to reconstruct what their role actually was. We can at least get an idea of how important it was from the degree of conflict it created, and the vehemence of the efforts to reduce women's influence. Two things are clear — one is that women played a very active part in missionary work and in the founding, organizing and nurturing of new churches. Some worked with husbands, others seem to have been either widows or single, but it is hard to tell. Lydia, for instance, is mentioned alone, and as in charge of her household. She might have been a widow running her husband's business, or a daughter carrying on her father's or an inheritor of enough money to start her own. She might even have been a married woman whose husband did not play an active role in the business or in her church activities. In any case these Christian women were accepted as leaders, prophets and teachers in the community.

The other thing which is clear is that this caused conflict right from the start. This was natural enough, since the liberated and active role of these women went against the cultural stream, even in the comparatively liberated Roman world. There, as in Judaic cities, the reaction against the freedom of women was strong in secular circles as well as religious. It was seen to undermine the proper order of things, and provoked strong denunciation and much fear. It must have been very upsetting to many men who joined the new faith. Indeed the fact that the freedom and leadership of women lasted as long as it did is fairly strong proof that the equal status of women was derived directly and unmistakedly from Jesus himself. No less a source could justify a thing so alien to both Jews and Gentiles. In the first flowering of new communities, with their strong sense of the Spirit's presence so much a part of community experience, the cultural conditioning could be, and was, overlaid, but it did not disappear, as the similar prejudice against non-Jewish Christians disappeared.

There is an important reason for this. The prejudice of the first, Jerusalem, church against treating Gentile converts as in any sense equals was consciously faced and dealt with. The detailed attention Luke gives to this conflict (using the story of the Roman centurion, Cornelius, as an example) shows that this was a difficult issue which was decided in favour of the Gentiles on the basis of the evidence that God poured out the Spirit as much on them as on Jews. The debate went on for years, even after a kind of compromise decision had been reached, but in the end the equality of Gentiles was fully accepted. In the case of the status of women the church never came to a point of conscious decision. There was no "test case", as in the story of Cornelius. There is no indication that the church ever really dealt openly with the matter at the level of principle and precedent, whether in the local church or at a gathering of teachers. Rather, when conflict arose it was dealt with ad hoc, according to the mind of the person or persons who happened to have authority, or to express the mind of the more influential members of the congregation. As the churches grew in number and size there were, naturally, more and more people in them who had not shared that experience of energy and vision which drove the first missionaries, and swept away their earlier cultural conditioning. The new members were glad to accept Christ, but did not necessarily want their whole lifestyle upset.

When a doctrine of liberation is preached to an oppressed group it is seldom that the women in the group are directly affected, and many women who were accepted into the churches along with middle-class husbands or fathers never expected any significant change in their status; certainly their menfolk did not expect it. This was far from being always the case, and there were many examples, then and later, of women individually drawn to Christianity because they sensed a possibility of being fully themselves; many of these became martyrs in the early persecutions, and that is how we know about them. Yet we have to acknowledge that increasingly this strong sense of personal calling and empowerment among the women was felt as a threat, and so we get those calls for restrictions to be applied to their activities. But if Paul, or some of his followers (depending on who you think wrote II *Timothy*) found it necessary to put down women with such a heavy hand, to demand their silence and subordination, that can only have been because they were known to be anything but silent and subordinate. There were women around visibly preaching and leading.

We have strong indication that the churches from which developed the teaching contained in the Gospel and Epistles of John (the Johannine churches) gave a great deal of honour to women. We have no direct evidence such as those messages of Paul to women co-workers, or Luke's references in *Acts*, but the fourth Gospel clearly expresses the experience of a church which was open to the apostolic mission of women. I referred to this in talking about the story of the Samaritan woman, who became an evangelist. In the same gospel, it is Martha and not Peter who first makes the great statement of faith: "I know that you are the Christ, the Son of God who was to come into the world". And it is Mary Magdalen, a longtime follower of Jesus, who first sees the risen Lord, and is the first witness to preach that good news, thus fulfilling the criteria given in *Acts* for being an apostle — to have been with Jesus in his earthly life, seen the risen Lord and borne witness to him. The reason for the different atmosphere which we can detect in the Johannine tradition is important. What distinguished these churches from the churches of the Jerusalem tradition and those founded by Paul is that the Johannine churches drew their sense of Christ's authority from the assurance of the direct involvement of the Spirit who dwelt in them, and whose presence they were to discern and test. While we need not say that they lacked organization — any group develops that — they did not set up such clear categories of leadership as the Pauline churches did. Paul had a respect for strong leadership — he was, after all, a Roman citizen, and it certainly helped to keep congregations together in the face of divisive influences. The Epistles of John, however, reflect a fear of subversive influences, but seem to assume that these cannot be countered simply by laying down the law, as Paul was inclined to do, and as the Jerusalem elders felt they had a right to do.

The Johannine churches became split, some amalgamated with the Pauline churches, some drifted towards degrees of gnostic doctrine, because they had no adequate model for decision-making, the only available one in that society being the hierarchical authority structure which rapidly developed in the mainstream church. This was based, in fact, on the model of Jewish synagogue officers, and later on Roman administrative models. But perhaps the Johannine churches were feeling their way towards a model of consensus decision-making, though they never had time to develop it efficiently. Consequently they suffered from divisions which they had no means to resolve. It is not merely coincidence that the only other considerable body of Christians which refused hierarchy and developed a consensus model was the Society of Friends, which has maintained an equality of the sexes in membership and ministry from the beginning, and has never had a category of leaders regarded as a special class. The Johannine churches did not manage to develop a model on these lines conscious enough to sustain itself, so it is not surprising that the strongly organized churches either absorbed them, or repelled them into obscurity. Clear-cut leadership and authority to make difficult decisions make for strength and survival, and those churches survived. By the second century their organization under single local bishops, presiding over a college of presbyters assisted by deacons, was firm and unquestioned.

All the authority roles, drawn from Jewish or Gentile models, were male. We see in the later epistles of Paul (including the famous interpolation in *1 Cor. 14:34-35*) only the faint rumblings of the antifeminine storm which was to sweep women from ministry and eventually from any great measure of respect as Christian persons, unless they were celibate and under the control of the bishop. (The other exceptions to their eventual degraded status as sub-Christians were through royalty or immense wealth.)

That story has been told many times, but the systematic degradation of a segment of human beings by other human beings is unfortunately not at all unusual. What is unusual, and worthy of celebration, is the fact that, as we have seen, there was a time when a very different situation prevailed. Men and women worked, prayed, suffered, and rejoiced together in Christ. They made all kinds of mistakes, they were angry, or proud, or mean, or deceitful — together. And they were heroic and visionary and compassionate, side by side. And it did not seem to them odd, nor did they do it in order to defy others or prove a point, but because it seemed natural and inevitable. It was just that sense of naturalness which was its downfall, for nobody bothered to justify what everyone experienced as right and proper, in the light of the gospel. So when the tide turned there were no articulate justifications ready to defend what had been discovered. Against the attacks of those armed with prejudice, precedent and spiritual texts, it had little chance.

But it happened. And it is important to notice that the time when it happened, like other times in history when women and men have loved one another as co-workers for the gospel, was a time when the Christian tradition was visibly and evidently true to the Spirit which informs that gospel. This has been especially marked in two kinds of situations — the frontier experiences of mission, and the experience of persecution.

It is a cherished part of American history that as the nation pushed westward the pioneering situation called on everyone, male or female, to take an equal share of the toil and hardship. Stories of heroic frontier women abound and among them stories of Christian women, including Catholic Sisters, who laboured in incredible conditions to bring health-care, a semblance of education, and some kind of human dignity to those who suffered from the worst feature of the pioneering spirit — the greed for money that grabbed what it wanted without mercy or foresight. The victims of the pioneering spirit were the native Americans, the prostitutes, the orphans, the destitute people who were lured by the hope of paradise but found only degradation. Into that situation came Christian women serving those victims. They were from many denominations, sometimes officially sent by the large churches as deaconesses, or nuns, or representatives of church organizations; sometimes they belonged to groups of women only, alternative organizations or movements alongside those run by men. Some have become legendary for their achievement, their courage, their humour and undaunted creativity, like Sister Blandina of Santa Fe who disarmed a lynch mob, and built a school to teach trades to local girls, though she had no assets except a strong will and an imagination that could make others see the visions she saw. Such women were accepted even by those who would in theory reject any claims of women to equality. The atmosphere they created somehow made the arguments irrelevant, at least at the time. In frontier towns, or among the immigrants in the slums of Chicago or New York or New Orleans, the sex of those who came there because that was where Christ called them did not seem to be an important issue. It was only when the vigour of these women's leadership, the extraordinary devotion they attracted, and the success that attended their work became obvious to those who controlled the churches that problems arose, and the struggle of Christian women for recognition had to be undertaken. Where the real work of the gospel was going on these questions were not even raised.

It was the same in the mission field. Just as in Germany, Gaul and the Celtic areas of Europe in the "Dark Ages", women like Bridget carried the message of Christ as freely as the men, so in Asia and Africa in the nineteenth-century women and men ventured together into new places. Their methods of evangelization and their attitudes to indigenous cultures may now seem narrow and bigoted, but their dedication and sincerity are unquestionable, and that was more important. Once more, in those places where church structures did not yet exist a Christian was simply a Christian, and there was neither Jew nor Gentile, male nor female.

The other situation in which the normal cultural separations of the sexes dissolve is that of persecution. The threat of imprisonment and death as the possible price of faith quickly relativizes concerns for social acceptability or domestic order as normally conceived. To name one historical example out of dozens, in England during the persecution of Catholics in the sixteenth or seventeenth century women who were householders were relied on as religious leaders; they organized and safeguarded the clandestine meetings of the faithful, devised means to pass the hunted priests from one "safe house" to another, and generally carried the responsibility for the morale and even the existence of the local congregation. They led and taught the faith. Their role (untitled but powerful) was accepted and even demanded, and as a result some of them, like Margaret Clitheroe, were tortured and killed. And it is one of the ironies of history that the earlier persecution of Protestants under Queen Mary called on men and women together to display an equal courage, to teach and preach together and sometimes to die together. In each case this companionship in witness contradicted the normal patriarchal structures of the church or sect to which these women belonged. In time of peace they would have been expected to be obedient wives or daughters, or silent and unobtrusive nuns, all under the unquestioned and traditionally hallowed control of men.

This androgynous Christian experience is evident in times of crisis and social dislocation, when for some reason (the absence of normal cultural patterns, as in mission territory, or their abrogation by the experience of persecution or disaster) the cultural pressures are removed. This experience is curiously expressed in the symbols which emerge from the very early post-apostolic Christian experience. In the gnostic Gospel of Thomas, which dates probably from the early second century, Peter protests to Jesus that Mary Magdalen should not be allowed to share in the secret teaching which belongs to the disciples of Jesus, since she is a woman. In this story, as we have seen, Mary Magdalen's name is that which stands for strong womanhood, it is she who encourages and exhorts the men in this apocryphal gospel and in others. In one, Levi defends her, even to the point of saying that "Jesus loves her more than us" because he knows her. And Jesus assures them that Mary can "become like you men". The cultural assumption is that the feminine is inferior, yet the *experience* of genuine life in Christ is that women — some at least — are far from inferior. The conclusion is that their spiritual transformation makes them "like men". This is the inevitable conclusion of a patriarchal society struggling to make sense of the obvious spiritual power and holiness of women, and it would be a mistake to dismiss it as just another example of the tendency to make the male the norm. It is that, of course, but the fact that such a weird conclusion is drawn shows how powerful was the experience that could only express itself in those terms.

It was internalized by the women also. Among the most famous of the early accounts of martyrdom are those concerning the suffering of Perpetua and Felicitas, one a patrician young woman, the other a slave, probably black. The emphasis in the story is almost entirely on the two women, especially Perpetua whose own account of her experience in prison is preserved, followed by an eyewitness account of the martyrdom. In prison, Perpetua dreams that she mounts a heavily-defended ladder and enters a beautiful garden where a man like a shepherd is milking sheep; he gives her some of the milk in her cupped hands (the way in which the eucharistic bread was received at that time.) This assures her of the victory to come, and a few days later she dreams that a friend of hers, the deacon Pomponius, leads her into the amphitheatre, telling her "do not be afraid, I am here struggling with you". Here already we see that in bearing witness to Christ, male and female are struggling together. Then, in the dream, instead of a wild animal, an "Egyptian" is let loose against her — a dark-skinned and "vicious-looking" person, who represents the power of evil. Then there come to her "some handsome young men" to be her seconds and assistants, and when her clothes are stripped off, "suddenly I was a man".

Perpetua triumphed in her dream, as some days later she did in real life, and for her the possibility of overcoming lay in the fact that her "feminine" weakness was transformed into the image of the victorious male. That is the symbol, but her role in the prison, in real life, is equally one of confident leadership. She can uphold and cheer the men who are to die, and when her father comes to plead with her she rejects, though with pity for him, the whole patriarchal system in which a daughter should respect, believe and obey her father above all. Even her baby, still at the breast, represents for her that which binds her to a world from which her faith has freed her. Her father tries to use her love for the child to get her to sacrifice to the gods, and her need for the baby is great; as she says, when he is with her the prison "seems like a palace". But she cannot keep the baby if the price is the loss of the wholeness and transcendance she has found. In the account which has come down to us, the baby is successfully weaned, her milk dries up. For her, maternity means subjection.

In Felicitas too, the call to martyrdom is a call beyond maternity, for that, in their eyes, ties a woman to a system in which the freedom of Christ is impossible. Felicitas' baby is born in prison, and adopted by a Christian woman, so that the mother, only just delivered, is able to be led to the beasts. The whole story (written by men) shows the complete acceptance of women as companions in suffering and witness, and shows them able to lead, to give example, to command. A woman can command, it seems, even beyond the grave, for Perpetua dreams of her little brother, who had died unbaptized, and sees him dirty and distressed, unable to reach the water of life. She prays earnestly and with confidence, and later dreams that the child is now healed, able to reach and drink the water, and to go and play in the garden of paradise.

Felicitas laboured in prison, and gave birth to a daughter, but also to her freedom. Patient and strong, she and her friend stood together in the arena, beside the men who were their friends and equals. Perpetua in her dream "became a man" and many times male writers writing admiringly of women have expressed this by saying that they had somehow left their femaleness behind. It is not a way of expressing the transforming experience that can appeal to women, yet it is important, now, to recognize that the thing itself is not new, that it has been part of the Christian experience from the beginning, at those moments when Christianity has been closest to that which Jesus himself drew on for his understanding of human potential. These are those moments when men and women are set free from the restrictions of systems designed to keep order and peace by separating people into exclusive categories, erecting barriers between them and keeping the barrier closed by means of conscious and unconscious fears. It was those barriers which Jesus experienced, and which he saw to be the cause of the sickness and suffering and poverty all around him. He lived and died and rose to break down those barriers. At the times when the barriers have been loosened or breached by cultural upheaval, as in our own time, it is possible to see that another way, his way, is real, that human beings can live and work together to create a different world.

We can put it differently: where we see men and women working side by side as friends, trying to care for and understand each other, to forgive each other, to free each other to serve those who are still unfree — there we see the sign of the kingdom which Jesus preached. There is a new creation, and Eve becomes the mother of all living. But when that happens, Perpetua and Felicitas need not choose between motherhood and freedom, their childbearing becomes a birth into new life for themselves and those who share with them. Then the experience can be expressed not as a woman becoming a man, but rather as a human being becoming a new person.

VIII. THE MOTHER

The most famous of all New Testament women is also the most enigmatic when we begin to ask questions about her as a credible human being. There are really two stories about Mary, mother of Jesus; one of these can possibly be put together from the four gospels and one reference in *Acts*, the other is the story of how Mary of Nazareth became the Theotokos, the God-bearer — bearer also of all the feminine symbols of Godhead and arguably the single most powerful influence on the art and culture of Western civilization. The second story is in many ways more interesting, and feminist studies have recently become fascinated by the weight of symbolism carried by the slender figure of Mary, and its importance in helping us to comprehend the underside of a patriarchal religious culture and the curious escapes it provided for itself. It has also been possible to realize how this figure, majestic and glorious in heaven, provided a way for inglorious and oppressed women to retain some sense of self-worth in spite of the pious manipulation, the constant attacks on their feminine integrity and consciousness, which were used by religious systems to keep them in a state of guilt and submission. The recovery of the half-forgotten yet powerful goddess whose image Mary has become through the centuries is also the theme of many modern studies, by men as well as women. It carries within it the hope of a saner and more honest social climate, with the promise of peace.

The last chapter in this book must concern itself with that second story to some extent, but first of all there is that other one, slighter and harder to write, of the real woman who disappears from the pages of Scripture with the same completeness and abruptness as the other women of the gospels. Her story is hard to write because it has become so entangled with the other one. Every gospel incident has been reinterpreted to make the image of Mary, mother of Jesus, fit the requirement of Mary, mother of God. Certainly, they are the same person, yet even a nodding acquaintance with Marian literature shows the writers (almost always male) beginning with the theologically developed picture of the Sinless One, the Second Eve, and then fitting the gospel incidents into it, even at the cost of amazingly complicated explanations of the text. When we add to the genuine theological development (however odd) the romantic compensations of St. Bernard and other male celibates, or the type of ideal Victorian female to which Mary was also accommodated (barely adult and quite incapable of any sexual feeling or indeed anything but passive resignation) then the image of Mary has clearly lost touch with any kind of human reality.

There has been another school of thought, more recently, which attempted to compensate for the almost invertebrate image of Mary by stressing her physical endurance, the hard labor as well as the grief and stress of her ordinary daily life. This sounds more "real", but Mary remains, in this version, still the ideal background, the good, laborious wife and sympathetic mother, the support and foil to the active Joseph and Jesus.

The big questions remain unanswered. They are really two very different questions, though they overlap. One is the obvious human question — on the available evidence, what kind of mother was Mary? This question has, of course, been asked and answered before, but it has generally been asked and answered in terms of a theology of Mary developed for quite other reasons: Mary must be the perfect mother because she *was* perfect, so the biblical evidence has been made to support this. It is not treated seriously as a source.

The other question is exegetical — what kind of figure do Luke, Matthew, and John respectively intend to evoke? The second question is really primary, since we cannot form an idea of what weight to give to the references as biographical material unless we know why and how the writers used their available material, not primarily for biographical purposes.

Matthew's infancy narrative is focussed on Joseph's call and predicament. For him Mary is the means for fulfillment of prophecy, her role is the typical woman's role of having things done to her — she conceives, she is to be rejected or not as her husband decides; she gives birth, she is taken to safety and brought home again. For Matthew, then, Mary is certainly significant as the means for divine action, and if we want to draw conclusions from his narrative about the kind of person she was we shall need a lot of imagination. About the only obvious inference is that she was physically tough and had a lot to put up with. (*Mt* 13:54-58, *Mk* 6:1-6) Matthew's two other references to her are parallel to Mark's. One occurs when the behaviour of the young man from Nazareth rouses surprise, since his background is so well known. "Isn't he the carpenter's son? Isn't his mother called Mary? And his brothers, James, Joseph, Simon and Jude? Aren't his sisters still here with us?" Mary is simply part of the expected background. The only extra bit of biographical information here is, by inference, that at the time of her son's public ministry Mary was a widow, for her husband is not mentioned.

Matthew's other reference is again paralleled in Mark, and also in Luke (*Mt* 12:46-50, *Mk* 3:31-35, *Lk* 8:19-21), and this is one of those stories which have taken a lot of explaining, because they appear to contain a rebuff to Mary, along with the rest of the family. When Jesus' relatives assert a claim to his attention on the ground of that relationship he sets the claim aside very firmly. "Who are my mother and kin? Here are my mother and family — those who do the will of my heavenly Father are my brothers and sisters and mother." The same lesson is brought home when a woman calls down blessings on the womb that bore him and the breasts that nursed him. "Rather, blessed are they who learn the word of God and keep it." Theologically, this attitude fits the emphasis in Mark, and in different ways in Matthew and Luke, on the harshness of the choices facing disciples who must be prepared to set aside even the dearest ties for the sake of the kingdom. Blood kinship is second to the deeper kinship of those who have been born to a new consciousness, and these passages make the point that Jesus himself did what he asked his disciples to do.

The biographical significance of these obviously important and well-remembered incidents is secondary for the evangelists, but it is helpful. We can put them together with reference in *Mark* (3:20-21) to the fact that at one point in the Galilean ministry Jesus was so driven by his need to respond to the suffering and neediness of the people that he and his disciples "had no chance to eat", and his family tried to "take charge of him" because he seemed to be going out of his mind. Evidently they did not succeed, but that reference adds to the general picture of the family's attitude to Jesus. It was protective and possessive. At a later time, when he seemed to hesitate about whether or not to go up to Jerusalem, his family urged him to go, evidently wanting him to make a public stand and unable to understand his doubts. Here we see that the family supported what they themselves conceived to be Jesus' public role. They were clear about it, and included themselves in it. They were, therefore, inclined to feel they had a right to advise and even direct him; they wanted to correct his imprudence or strengthen his weakness. And Mary, his mother, was for a time at least explicitly and implicitly involved in this family system.

The idea that Mary was part of the grouping of her own family, rather than that of the converted, is borne out by the fact that she is only mentioned once with the latter. It is only John who mentions her presence with two others at the cross, and John's reasons for placing the mother at the foot of the cross are special to him and important for us. I have touched on them in an earlier chapter but there is one aspect which is especially relevant here. John-bar-Zebedee's special relationship with the mother of Jesus was evidently well-known, and John mentions its justification in the words of the dying Jesus, consigning his mother to the care of his closest male friend, but also consigning the man to the care of the woman, as mother. The man and the woman, the male and female disciples, are united under the cross. But there is a curious implication here. Are we also witnessing the reconciliation of Jesus' mother with his "little flock"? Was Mary, at some point, rejected by her family? Their notion of the Messianic campaign had clearly failed, yet she would not leave her son. Did John receive her from Jesus — and thus run into trouble later with some of the other apostles who resented the family's attitude? Even more poignantly — was that moment beneath the cross a moment of reconciliation between a mother and son who had been estranged?

John's other story about Mary (*John* 2:1-11) may help towards an understanding. The story of the wedding feast at Cana is another of the incidents which have provided headaches for those who feel that the relationship between mother and son must, on theological grounds, have been smooth and intimate. It is altogether a very odd story, and recent scholars have suggested that it is in fact two stories woven together. One of them is the great sign of the water become wine, the sign which occurs on the "third day" of the new time symbolically inaugurated by the proclamation of John the Baptist. The power of Jesus to transform is a theme of John's gospel: the Christ transforms human beings into "offspring of God", he changes water to wine, doubt to faith, blindness to sight; his body becomes transforming food, and from that body in death flow the signs of regeneration, water and blood. And it all begins at a wedding, the very symbol of Israel's relationship with her God — the new Israel is transformed by the wine of the true vine, the life-blood of her bridegroom.

All of this does not seem to require the presence of Mary, but it seems very likely, in the nature of family celebrations and relationships, that she was indeed present on that occasion. It is also fitting that John should discern a role for her in the making of the sign, as he had portrayed her standing by the cross from which flowed the blood of the Lamb John the Baptist had proclaimed. Again the theology and the biography are inextricable. But the second story sounds more like another of those family rejection incidents preserved in the written and oral sources used by Mark and Luke. In it, Mary tried to tell Jesus what to do and was told bluntly that she had misunderstood the situation and should not interfere. Yet the story as told by John does not end there, for Jesus does in fact go on to do as she asked, and so give the first sign which "revealed his glory and led his disciples to believe in him".

There is something much stranger going on here than either a straight conflict between an ambitious and insensitive mother and a son striving to identify his vocation (as some have suggested), or the older interpretation of the son's response, beyond expectation, to his mother's trust. John wove what looks like a rejection story (which was of no theological interest to him) into one of his great "sign" stories. The only reason for him to do that which seems to make sense is that the sign he wanted to proclaim occurred in a human context which also did contain a rejection. But the way the rejection happens in his version is special, because this time it is not simply a matter of putting family ties and family expectations second. The discussion assumes a common ground between Jesus and his mother. Her expectation is that he will act within the terms of the Messianic character she assigns to him, for one of the chief characteristics of the Messianic kingdom is abundance of food and drink, an end to want. She is saying, in effect, "Now is your chance to show who you are." He does not reject her understanding of his role or his power, nor even her right to prompt him. He simply tells her that the occasion is inappropriate, the plight of the wedding party is not his — nor her — concern. "My hour is not yet come," — the time of glorification. Afterwards he seems to conclude that maybe she was right, and acts accordingly. It is all very odd. What we seem to be witnessing, through the mixture of traditional sources and John's theological filter, is an encounter between two strong and opinionated people, an encounter based on a common ground of much shared reflection and understanding, yet showing signs of stress, division and misunderstanding.

So far then, we have more than hints of a complex relationship in which, for some time at least, an estrangement developed. After the wedding at Cana, John says that Jesus "went down to Capernaum in company with his mother, his brother and his disciples." This was before the days of notoriety. Capernaum became, at some point, his home, and evidently it was his mother's home too, where she lived with other family members who had at some point left Nazareth. Yet a little later we find Jesus staying not with them but in Simon's house, and refusing to allow his family to claim him or dictate to him. Much later still, his mother is in Jerusalem apparently unsupported by any family members. Yet after Pentecost we find family members in prominent positions in the new assembly, though Mary is not mentioned.

It seems possible that Luke's infancy narratives can give us some clues about the background to these divisions and changes. Luke's first two chapters are something like a separate gospel, different in style and matter from the rest. His sources were unlikely to have included eyewitnesses even in a corroborative sense, though a dating of Luke in the late 60's would make it just possible for living testimony to have been available. These stories were current, it seems, among a limited group, for Matthew evidently drew on a different corpus of infancy stories, though with obvious overlapping. Wherever this group was located it was one in which the role of women was appreciated. It may be, as Geoffrey Ashe has proposed, in his very intriguing book, *The Virgin*, that the group which preserved the infancy stories used by Luke was actually one which had gathered around Mary herself as an older woman, and revered her as a teacher and prophet. In any case the stories which Luke obtained allowed him (or possibly compelled him) to see the main "speakers" — Mary, Elizabeth, Zachariah and Simeon, as prophetic characters in the great tradition of Israel. But Mary is the center of the narrative. Unlike Matthew's version, Luke's story is the gospel of Mary. She is the inspired vessel of God's action, and the other prophecies cluster around her role. The great canticle of Mary is modelled on the thanksgiving canticle of Hannah, mother of Samuel, when she found herself pregnant after years of barrenness, and Mary's virginity, as well as the long barrenness of Elizabeth, recalls the other childless women of Scripture who conceive at God's command, — Sarah, Rebecca, and Rachel, mothers of the patriarchs. Mary in Luke is very conscious of the tradition in which she stands, and of its great fulfillment in her own body. The canticle interprets God's action in her as explicitly Messianic. God will feed the hungry, exalt the poor, and humiliate the rich and powerful, as he has promised, and his promise is sure. Moreover, she herself is not just its passive vessel but its active servant. "He that is mighty has done great things for me". She had been lowly but is lifted up, and she is not afraid to claim the blessedness which is hers.

Again, theology and biography merge. The canticle is a formal composition, but the apparently irrelevant details of the narrative make us realize that we are also in touch with memories, the stories told and retold by those who saw and heard and wanted others to know and remember. Mary, after the angel's visit, set out and went "with haste" to visit her cousin, impatient to share with this other chosen one the extraordinary experience which she was struggling to understand. Was it in the conversation between the two women that the form of the divine message to Mary became clearly articulated? It took a form that expressed the essence of the ineffable experience in words that related it to the history and hope of their people. The narrative of Annunciation became a prophetic proclamation.

The time of the census came, and the mother, jolted for days over rough roads, gave birth unexpectedly early, with no time for adequate preparation, but she "wrapped him in swaddling clothes", a phrase which surely was a detail remembered by a woman. There was nothing strange about it, all babies were wrapped in swaddling clothes, but perhaps somebody who saw it told it in those words, creating a vivid and intimate mental image which has endured. The ordinariness of the scene is the key to its meaning: — "wrapped in swaddling clothes and lying in a manager", the shepherds found him.

And his mother "treasured all these things and pondered them in her heart". The sentence tells us that Mary was remembered as a person who reflected deeply, but also as a person whose reflections were shared; at some point she shared the awesome words of Simeon's prophecy which foretold deliverence for the people but rejection for the child and pain for the mother. Perhaps it was retold later to friends and followers, by a woman looking back and longing to reach an understanding through hindsight of the tragedy which had engulfed her. Simeon, it seems, perceived a tragic role for Mary and her son in contradiction to the glory and triumph welcomed by Zachariah, and by the canticle of Mary herself. Were those ill-omened words only added later to a corpus of stories whose keynote was joy and hope? Was there a retelling, a need to perceive, even in those earliest signs, the tragedy which had followed? There is a hint of what of what was to come in the peculiar story of Jesus' first Passover, when, now become "a man in Israel", he travelled to Jerusalem, and worshipped for the first time with the men in the Court of Israel, leaving his mother outside in the Court of the Women. Later, absorbed by new ideas and experiences, he stayed behind, perhaps spending the night with new friends so as to return to the Temple schools early the next day. Ignoring everything but his own absorbing hunger for wisdom, and the questions that sprouted in his mind, he took the first steps away from his family, and his mother. It all fits.

Luke presents Mary as a prophetess, and it seems very likely that Mary saw herself in that role. Far from the humble, submissive maiden of pious literature, she comes through as strong, excitable and militant. She had learned from her family to cherish the Messianic hopes of her people, to pray urgently for their fulfillment. She had felt the quickening tide of expectation which swept through the country, and she believed that at last the promise was fulfilled, in herself. So, apparently, did her family. The thing had to be played down, kept secret — the political threat of such a child was obvious, as the Herod story makes clear, but it was a family secret. Jesus' mother, with the inner circle of his family, believed him to be the destined Messiah, and believed they had the job of making sure he lived up to it. We get the impression that some reserved judgment and were very ready to drop him if he didn't turn out to be adequate Messiah material. A woman like Mary, mystical, courageous, intuitive and a born leader, committed her whole life to the calling which she had received, and interpreted it as well as she could, reading Scripture, reflecting, talking it over with intimates, and , as he grew, with Jesus himself. As the widow of one who was probably a landless younger son she had little status, and as the glorious babyhood memories became distant it seemed harder to keep the hope alive. As the years passed, since all those who had shared the experience of those days were distant or dead, it may be that she even doubted her own experience.

But John the Baptist began to preach, a wave of expectation swept the people once more, swept Nazareth also and Jesus with it, and she knew the time had come. He was away for months, and when he came back he was different, rather remote. To her the matter was still simple — he was the one, the need was urgent, the time had come, he had only to declare himself. For him, since his weeks in the desert, the whole thing looked different, problematic, vivid yet unclear. He was feeling his way into a vocation different from anything he or she had imagined. It was at this point that the encounter at Cana brought the conflict into the open.

Naturally, we can find no certainty about an incident which reaches us in a form modified by so many imponderable influences, but work in Scripture in recent years has been inclined to credit biblical authors with more discretion and less arbitrariness in handling their sources than it was once popular to ascribe to them. We can perceive that a story like this was not at all likely to have been either invented, or so altered as to lose touch with the genuine memories of those who were there, or at least heard what happened at the time. We do have here the story of a human encounter of great importance for the people involved, whose symbolic significance, later discerned, made it an unforgettable element of the preaching in one particular church at least.

We have a few converging bits of evidence to help us weigh the significance of the Cana story in helping us penetrate the enigma of Mary. One is the fact, already referred to, that John's gospel was written for, and in the context of, a church that was accustomed to giving an important role to women. Then we have the notion that Mary came to have a special relationship with John-bar-Zebedee, who was, if not the author of the whole of John's gospel, at least the source of the tradition, and probably author of those parts which are story rather than theological reflection. (John A.T. Robinson was not alone, however, in believing that the whole of John's gospel might be dated before A.D. 70. It seems likely enough that much of it was indeed very early with some editing and theological "framing" provided later.) If John-bar-Zebedee is shown as taking on a special responsibility for the mother of Jesus (whom John's gospel never refers to by name) that may be a way of "theologizing" the fact that Mary was rejected by the Jerusalem Church and found a place — personally and theologically — in the development of a church that was able to handle the notion of women's discipleship without discomfort. It may even be due to her influence that this trend developed as it did. The "beloved disciple", closest to Jesus and most in touch with his thinking and feeling, became at some point the leader and inspiration of a church that diverged in important ways from the Jerusalem Church, and the Pauline churches. It is not coincidence that this was also the church where the role of women as Jesus delineated it was less controversial.

It seems very likely, in fact, that the division which took place did find its root in the whole question of the role of women. If the Lucan account — presumably the official Jerusalem account — of the early days of the church leaves out all mention of women who had been prominent only days before, that is not accidental. John's church wrote no such account of its early days (or if it did it was lost) but we have the indirect evidence of John's gospel that the mother of Jesus was at least an honoured figure in it, and as we saw Mary Magdelene is also given the role of prophet of the resurrection. At some point the patriarchal leadership of the Jerusalem church clashed with the leadership claims of the women whom Jesus had called and commissioned as messengers of good news.

The supposition of a power-struggle in the Jerusalem church which involved a split over the role of the women is supported by the negative evidence, as we have seen. The role of Jesus' family, some of whom eventually became prominent in the church, could have been expected to include a role for the mother of Jesus, but since she is not mentioned it seems likely that the rift which had occurred between her and the rest when she refused to abandon her son in his failure was not fully healed, and that after the resurrection Mary identified herself more with the other women disciples with whom she had shared that bitter experience. It seems likely that some of the women, including the mother of Jesus and Mary of Magdala, found a sphere of ministry in the group inspired by the teaching of the beloved disciple. It may be that it was from this group, wherever located at the time, that some of them set out as missionaries to Gaul, where the mission of the Pauline and Jerusalem churches had not yet penetrated. But by then the mother of Jesus would have been too old, or perhaps too absorbed in the work she had. Or perhaps she was already dead. If so, nobody knows where she was buried, there are no relics, no pilgrimages. She disappeared totally — but paradoxically she became increasingly present.

The body of the mother of Jesus is the source of vast theological growth through the centuries. Her virginity, proclaimed by Luke as an aspect of her prophetic role, is reflected on as time goes on, and its significance embroidered for quite different reasons. The immaculate one, the one raised up to heaven, free of all taint of corruption in her flesh, is a very ambiguous sign. On the one hand, for the conscious purposes of the patriarchal establishment, she is the exalted and separate but wholly passive vehicle of divine will, purified in order to provide a source of human life for her son, untainted by sex. On the other hand she is a marvelous focus for male celibate fantasy, the romantic Lady about whom one can be passionate without danger; some of the prayers and praises addressed to Mary by her male devotees have been very erotic indeed and have also attributed to her a power and glory not short of divinity except in name. But she is also, apparently quite uncontrollably, a goddess-figure, the feminine divinity denied by Judaism and Christianity. She grows and grows, larger and larger in mosiac and painting and sculptured glory, more and more powerful in doctrine, liturgy and popular devotion. Feasts cluster around her, legends and visions proliferate.

The Church through the centuries was haunted, even dominated at every moment, by the woman it rejected. The official church became quite schizoid in its response — on the onehand promoting and approving more and more shrines and devotions with more and more elaborate theological justification for them: Mary is co-redemptrix with her Son, her intercession is all-powerful. On the other hand she is emphatically human; creature, not creator; utterly separated from the source of divine power which bestows glory on her. She becomes also a means to keep women in their subordinate place, for it is pointed out that with all her glory, she is always obedient, she is not "ordained", she is the busy but submissive, patient and suffering auxiliary who can intercede but not decide: the ideal priest's house-keeper.

There is another side to the cult of Mary, however, an unintended subversive tendency with regard to the role of women. Here is this figure, crowned and regal, sitting above the altar. In those Latin cultures where "machismo" is strongest and women are most oppressed there also are the most regal symbols of Mary. She is the queen, she is lifted up and alone. She is not identified by her relationship with a male, for even if she has her baby on her lap he is not the important one, he is sometimes almost hidden by her robes; she reigns alone, powerful to gain blessings and relieve sorrow. This is not a liberating image for poor women, but it does provide a means of spiritual and psychological survival. Within the oppressive system created by men, there is this sacred friend who is too strong to be oppressed; the male clergy think she is on their side but she is not. Single and sovereign, she yet allies herself with the dependent and rejected, and can inspire the inner strength and dignity to resist to destruction of soul as well as body.

Related to this women's "underground resistance" symbolized by Mary, is a less easily identified trend which was celebrated by Carl Jung, who saw in the dogma of the Assumption of Mary a sign that the feminine consciousness was breaking through the crust of patriarchal culture in both religious and secular spheres. Certainly the proclamation of that dogma coincided with the beginnings of a new surge in feminist consciousness. The women's cause had for a while seemed to be "merely" a demand for equal civil rights for women, but it was opposed by church and state with an hysterical intensity and malice attributable only to a subconscious awareness of a deep threat to the whole male culture. Yet the very experience of working for admittance to male rights and roles raised women's consciousness to a point where something else began to break through: the "women's movement" as such was born, and the symbol of Mary rose along with it. Mary is the "woman-identified" woman, whole in herself (immaculate) capable of maternity without a male (virgin, yet mother), and she is shown raised to the heart of the hitherto "male" Trinity, completing it, yet curiously disturbing its "maleness" so that it becomes impossible to ignore the divine feminine. Suddenly theologians rushed to explain that "Spirit" in Hebrew is feminine, that there is much feminine symbolism even around Yahweh, that Sophia, divine Wisdom (feminine in Hebrew and Greek) is the "power of God" and identified at different times with the Law (Torah) with the Christ, and with Mary. The symbols slide over each other, it is all quite confusing. What is clear is that the proclamation of the Assumption symbolized and perhaps triggered uncontrollable forces, the same forces at work in the very heart of the religious world as were being released in the secular world. Perhaps even, unconsciously, the proclamation and all its attendant worship was an attempt to placate a resurgent and vengeful goddess, and keep her manageable.

It seems as if, after all, there is a real connection between the historical person, Mary of Nazareth, and the cultic figure of the Mother of God. The very young church found it hard to deal with her, because she was part of Jesus' family but also mainly because she was a woman, a woman of strong personality and power of leadership. It seems she could not become a leader of a house-church, or a missionary, as many other women did, because her peculiar status as the mother of Lord complicated the way people related to her — one-time leader of of the family faction, but no longer so. She "disappeared" — but she disappeared into the unconscious of Christianity, and reappeared in due course in the form of dreams, visions and projections.

The Second Vatican Council of the Roman church made an attempt to "withdraw the projection" by refusing to deal with Mary as a separate object of theological investigation, trying rather to consider her as part of God's people, involved in and symbolizing the church. That would have been excellent if the implication of such a theological development for the role of the feminine in the church had been addressed. In practice, after a lot of uplifting rhetoric, absolutely nothing was done to change the status of Christian women, and the masculine ethos of that church was, if anything, hardened by the removal of much Marian art and devotion from normal use, and (a small but significant detail) by the removal at the same time of the names of women saints from the Roman Canon of the Mass. The compensatory safety outlets for feminine consciousness were thus blocked, with predictable explosive results. The girl who knew herself blessed among women and foresaw the raising up of the lowly was fighting back.

We shall never know with much certainty about the relationship between Jesus and Mary, but at least we know it was real, strong, conflictual, loving, painful, and finally triumphant. We shall never know much for certain about the role of Mary in the early church, except that it was, once more, stormy, important, passionate and full of suffering. As for the relationship between the church and the symbol of the Mother of God, that is the most painful, ambiguous and conflictual of all. The Protestant churches could not stomach her, the Anglican tradition accorded her a polite but warm respect, the Catholic church both exalted and tried to neutralize her. Meanwhile, the power of the feminine divine principle, the Mother of God (or Mother Goddess) worked in its own way. As Catholic books on Marian subjects dwindle, the literature on the goddess swells, and many of the writers are well aware of the intimate relationship between the two.

For the Christian woman, the questions around the person of Mary are very near the heart of faith, for they concern a woman's response to the human reality of Jesus of Nazareth, in this case the response of the woman nearest of all to him. It seems as if the reality of Mary's own experience of calling was itself the source of her difficulties in relating to her son's own sense of mission. She was not, like the other women we encounter in the gospels, liberated by him — rather she encountered him, lived and grew with him, as a woman already liberated and affirmed by God's power. This is very close to the experience of some women now, who were brought up with a "sin-redemption" type of spirituality in which it was required that a person (more especially a woman) experience herself as sinful and helpless in order to be forgiven. But for many women the experience of healing and self-acceptance has come not through religious channels but through the women's movement. For such women, even those who continue to love their faith and long to find meaning in it, it is difficult to find a way to relate to the male religious figure of Jesus of Nazareth. The struggle to relate to him is painful and draining, full of alternating guilt and anger, longing and pride. Some cannot find a way to resolve the contradictions. They are driven to reject Jesus who has become only a hypocrite, an attractive but deceptive symbol of male domination. Some come through it, discovering in the end that a meeting is possible, a reconciliation can happen that is deep and integrating, but one which opens up depths of suffering, and entails the spiritual risks of vulnerability. It carries with it the likelihood of misunderstanding both from religious people and from feminist, but it is fruitful, it is a way of wholeness.

This, or something very like it, may have been the experience of Mary, mother of Jesus. It seems strange, yet appropriate, that modern women in that struggle for self-awareness and honesty should be able to turn for companionship and understanding to the first of all women to experience in all its painfulness and hope the enigma of Jesus, called Christ.

IX.
A TIME OF BIRTH

The stories of women with Jesus are stories about power. They are stories of the empowerment of those without power. The crucial question is, what kind of power is this? Our world is approaching the character of a hell because of the thirst for power of groups who regard the defeat or extinction of other groups as necessary to their own progress and prosperity. This applies to the attitude of the dominant human groups toward non-human life and matter, an attitude which, unchecked, will ensure that even if the world escapes nuclear destruction in pursuit of dominance by one group over another, life will be gradually (but quite rapidly) extinguished through the destruction of soil, water and air. This is power as we normally think of it, the power to control another or others, to use the other for one's own purposes. This is the power which regards the other as a separate thing, whose condition (apart from usefulness to the owner) is not relevant to the being of the power-user. It is power as conceived since the Renaissance. Bacon, spokesman for the new attitude, spoke of making nature a slave and "torturing her secrets from her"! Since then, the aim of science has been to find ways to dominate and control "nature", which is viewed as feminine.

But we live in an age when, finally, science, once the great justifier of that kind of power, has been driven to admit that its underlying assumption is invalid. In physics, in ecology, in economics, in biology, there is a growing realization that those who use power in such a way are signing their own death warrants, because we are all (and the "all" includes all matter, the whole earth) so deeply interrelated that we cannot exist without each other. As Fritjof Capra, himself a physicist, expressed it in his book, *The Turning Point*, in contrast to the mechanistic Cartesian view of the world, the world view emerging from modern physics can be characterized by words like organic, holistic, and ecological. "The universe is no longer seen as a machine, made up of a multitude of objects, but has to be pictured as one, indivisible, dynamic whole whose parts are essentially interrelated and can be understood only as patterns of a cosmic process."*

This is not a view that commends itself to those who profit from an economic system based precisely on that mechanistic model, which enables one group to treat another, or the earth, as a piece of machinery to be used and abused as convenient. It is not the view of that section of the scientific establishment which clings to the older models, models which give such a sense of god-like power to the human mind. It is not the view of the patriarchal culture as a whole which is constructed as a model of dominance, and the power of one group over the others — the women, the old, the weak, the land itself, even when that dominance is supposedly exercised for the benefit of the other.

The view expressed by modern physicists and others is (as has been noted with satisfaction or with disdain) closely related to mystical traditions, Eastern and Western. Forced by a global crisis, the terror of destruction by war or pollution, human beings are re-discovering an awareness that has been the province of a few wise people, but has not normally been applied in the areas of politics and common life. Jesus not only held such a view but he applied it forcefully and practically. His view of power was indeed that of the operation of a "cosmic process" with which he was on intimate terms. But this power was one which worked essentially in and through the hearts and minds of human beings, not controlling and dictating but inviting. It was power as empowerment. It liberated the power of the cosmic process within each one, but with that experience came the realization that the power released was essentially a shared one, and experience of relatedness.

In these stories we have been in touch with empowered women, very real human beings struggling to make sense of an undeniable experience of self and others, in the midst of a society that denied them any sense of self, or relatedness, except as it suited the purpose of the masters.

This is the story of women at all times who have touched the springs

*Fritjof Capra '*The Turning Point*' 1982 p. 66.

of God, suffered change, and then had to deal with a world that denied validity to the feminine, unless it could "become male". This story of the quest of women for freedom to grow from within themselves is not merely, as it can easily seem, the story of the struggle of women for a better life for themselves and other women. It is the struggle of the human race for its own spirit. In a patriarchal society women are those who are able, sometimes, to perceive an alternative, because — like the women who followed Jesus — they have nothing to gain from mere changes of power structures. Whoever wins in the male world of power, they will always lose, and with them all those who cannot or will not seize power and use it to control and exploit. The women are in touch with the decision of a potential Messiah who refused the possibility of gaining power by magical control over nature, by spectacular feats, or by sheer political skill. He chose not to be powerful in that sense, knowing that it was imcompatible with his experience of the Father. This was the God he called "Abba" in the child's affectionate diminutive name, because, paradoxically, this Fatherhood undermined and dethroned the divine Patriarch created by a patriarchal society in its own image. The Abba of Jesus denied the title of "Father" to anyone on earth, and taught that all were sisters and brothers — and mothers — to Jesus and to each other. But not "fathers". Jesus dethroned the role of male power. Instead, and because of his refusal to exercise that kind of power, the power of the dynamic divine energy flowed in and through him, and empowered all those who opened themselves to it. The liberating power in Jesus is the power of cosmic process, the life-giving of the Abba. The women who received that power were free to perceive the mission of Jesus and to live it.

Recently it has been possible for some privileged people to see the exhibit called "The Dinner Party", to which I referred in the introduction. It was designed by Judy Chicago, with a large number of other women and men and carried out by them in all kinds of embroidery and ceramic techniques. It has been shown in several places, but is presently (as far as I know) back in its packing cases, waiting for the aquisistion of a permanent site. The difficulty in finding places to exhibit, even for a while, and the even greater difficulty in obtaining money for a permanent exhibit is a sign of the attitude of the artistic establishment to anything that concerns women. (The story of women in the arts — the denial of opportunity, the forced anonymity, the attribution of their works to male artists, the refusal of exhibition and performance, and the strength and persistence with which some women found ways to create in spite of persecution and ridicule, is another heroic chapter in the story of women's quest for life.)

The exhibition consists of a huge dinner table built as a hollow triangle, and on the three sides are place-settings for thirty-three representative women, beginning with mythical female figures of pre-history and extending to the heroines of our own time. Each one is remembered not just for her personal achievement but for her influence on or work for women and for others. Each is represented symbolically on her own ceramic plate, and the embroidered runner on which it rests. Each is a work of art, the embroidery representing many styles of needlework in history. Each expresses the times, experience and being of the woman. The plates, worked over for months and often through many failures, evoke each woman distinctly, but most express the power and meaning of the person through feminine symbols evoking the openness of the womb, the source of life.

The theme of the whole is, indeed, a theme of power, but it is the power to give life, to influence and inspire and liberate through compassion, insight, courage, integrity. It is the power that springs from the acceptance of vulnerability, the fruit that grows from vision nurtured by patient endurance, refusing to die, proclaiming its message in spite of all. It is not possible to evoke in print the scope and meaning of powerful visual symbols, and for most people the nearest they can get to that experience is through the two volumes which commemorate the exhibition. These books tell and illustrate the amazing story of the creation of "The Dinner Party", and record the transformation wrought in the makers of it — experience of conversion and growth beyond all expectations. But the fruit of that long, bitter, triumphant struggle was to be seen in the effect of the exhibit on those who came to see it. The great room in which the table was set was very quiet and subdued. Couples, men and women, women together or women alone, moved quietly from one place-setting to another, and when they spoke it was in whispers. Some stood a long time, gazing, absorbing, perhaps puzzled or questioning, evidently moved. There was what can only be described as a sense of awe: a little fear, a longing, a peace, yet a disturbing challenge. For some, the explicitly female genital imagery was disturbing, yet undeniably appropriate, and combined with the evocation of real and often tragic experiences of the past to stir in the spectators a sense of compassion, but also of pride, challenge, hope, even dedication.

The fact that it is possible in our time for women to identify with such a proclamation of women's achievement, suffering, and identity, and for many men to share that experience, is one of the many signs of what is happening in our time. This possibility is the reason why it matters for us to recognize in all this the same thing which sprang to life among the women who followed Jesus. In making that connection lies the possibility for Christian women now to claim their heritage, to share it with those who hear the same sound of hope, and challenge the deathly intent of the dominant social reality of our time. We look to the women of the New Testament and find in them the companions and friends, the foremothers and sisters of the oppressed in our world.

To do that we have had to struggle to disinter the women of the New Testament from the graves of male assumptions in which they were buried some two thousand years ago. We have to undertake a kind of literary and religious dig, gently and skillfully uncovering the accumulated layers of Christian interpretation of Scripture, piecing together the scant remaining evidence. It is not much, but with skill, honesty and imagination it is enough.

We disinter these stories from the ruins of the patriarchial culture of the time of Jesus, and later. We find them, and try to understand them, in and through documents written by men. In this, the New Testament is no different from any other surviving literature. With very minor exceptions, reality has always been presented to us in the terms which made sense to the male mind, one which takes for granted the validity and fundamental naturalness of patriarchal culture. The few women writing within such a culture, their minds formed by it, tend to take it as given as much as the men. Though they have often been aware of the penalty imposed on their sex by it, they have not questioned it too much until the emergence of early feininists of the late eighteenth century. To write about women using only documents of this kind presents problems, some of which have been encountered in this book. I have not dealt at length with the technical methods required for this cultural dig; rather I have drawn on the results of others' skill. I have tried, with some of the products of their labor, to be in touch with the historical reality of certain women, evoking their experience to envision and challenge ours. The writing of this book leads finally to the point indicated by the emergence of a different consciousness in our time, one linked to the experience of women.

That point is the realization that the plight of women, such as those women Jesus freed and sent on missions, is not *one* of the major evils of our culture, past and present, or of any known culture. It is not one of the major evils because it is actually the only one.

It is the only one in the sense that the attitude of mind which countenances the routine subjection and oppression of women is the same attitude which regards domination and exploitation as the natural mode of human relationship to any other being at all. It is the attitude which could regard as normal and necessary the institution of slavery, and the enslavement of anything which serves the pursuit of power. It is easy, looking at the oppression and exploitation of whole categories of people — ethnic minorities, the poor in any country, or any race — to say that oppression is only incidentally a women's issue, that men and women are equally oppressed, and this is true, though it is also true that women are "the oppressed of the oppressed". But the basic attitude which permits or requires exploitation of one group by another is essentially the "masculine" power,in women as much as in men,that claims rights over those it can coerce.

But that is actually a position of fear. The position of dominance is, as modern science and ancient mysticism both suggest, based on a lie about reality, a lie about the nature of life. It is therefore extremely vulnerable and fragile, and constantly (though unadmittedly) afraid of being betrayed, undermined, exposed. The greater the fear, the greater the ferocity of the oppression. Unchallenged patriarchy can afford to be relatively benign; a hint of challenge provokes savage suppression by emotional as well as physical means. And always the deepest, most frightening challenge is that of the women. They are close to home, in the home, yet they are the "other", they represent and touch the feminine in each one, they expose the weakness in the dominant class. They are the enemy within the gates. That is why the signature of a patriarchal culture is prostitution, in which women can be controlled, used, degraded, and blamed, all at once. We live in a culture in which prostitution is accepted as inevitable and necessary, even rather amusing. "Torture" is not too strong a word for the repeated rapes and beatings and other abuses used to "toughen" a likely girl for her job of prostitution, but this treatment of girls, and women, even children, in this extremely lucrative trade is not of great interest to church or state, except, of course, that the officials of both make use of the services provided.

Prostitution sums up in action what our society thinks about the "other", the one who is weaker.

Estimates vary, but it seems that at least one in every ten women will be raped some time in her life. Some estimates say one in four. One in four girls under eighteen will be victims of incest, and of boys under fourteen, one in seven, since young boys are "feminine" too to this mentality. In most cases, the father (or stepfather, boyfriend, uncle, etc.) is the one who deprives a child of childhood, and spoils her life. Prostitution is a common fate of the incest victim, or else a shifting from man to abusive man, and the birth of children themselves fated to be abused.

All this is not some unusual tragedy of poverty and ignorance, it is the commonplace of every class in western society, it is what goes on in the homes of professionals and academics as well as unemployed laborers. It is the social worker's bread and butter. It is what our culture expects, it is the revenge of the masculine which feels its power threatened, which cannot do what it has claimed to do, cannot control what it needs to control, knows deep down and angrily that it is not God. And if I focus here on the treatment of women in Western society, it is not because the rest of the world treats them much better. There are degrees, from the routine sexual mutilation of girls in some Islamic countries and others, to their comparative emancipation (but always in subordinate roles) in communist countries, and in Scandinavia. The world picture is patriarchal. The differences lie in degrees of brutality in enforcing this system and the degree to which some women can by strength, wealth and cunning break into the system at various levels.

The overall pattern is constant. The scapegoat, the natural victim, is the woman. She represents what a patriarchal culture fears — the uncontrollable, the unpredictable, the source of life itself, the vulnerability which is also at the heart of the male person at the point where domination fails and life begins. But life cannot be controlled, though it can be destroyed.

In this last chapter, therefore, there is a need to ask what it was that Jesus did for women in his time which remains relevant for women now, and through them for our world. The women's song written for the strike of 1912 is perfectly correct: "The rising of the women is the rising of the race." The study of New Testament women is finally worthwhile not for historical interest but because unless we can understand them, not merely with our heads but with a gut feeling of empathy, we cannot realistically interpret and live the gospel in our time. This seems like a large claim, but it is basic to the thesis of this book; it is one with the statement that the attitude of our world, (*including* that of many of the women in it) to women is the point of condemnation and death or redemption and life.

There are no short cuts. Some liberation theologians, leaders of movements for freedom of minorities, and civil rights advocates feel we should go ahead and achieve liberation for the poor, the oppressed, and then worry about the women's issues. But if the attitude to women within the oppressed group is one which accepts their subordination and abuse, then that group's own understanding of liberation, and of the social relationships which make it possible to live freedom, are rotten at the roots and will rot the new order as it rotted the old.

The church, historically, lost touch with what Jesus did for women. It did not understand the centrality of his action for and with them, and therefore lost touch with his whole missionary thrust of liberation and empowerment of the poor. We can trace this historically, but we can also see that the results of the re-patriarchalization of Christianity were never total, the gospel proved resistant to suppression in the women who heard it. But it has taken a long time and much suffering and hindsight for us to get to the point where we can truly understand, as human beings looking to the gospels for hope, what kind of thing Jesus was doing.

In the time of Jesus, Jewish law protected women to some extent from the grosser forms of abuse, and there were, then as always, women whose personal qualities, or wealth, or education and connections, or the sensitivity of whose male relatives, enabled them to transcend this status of possession, in fact if not in law. There were many women in Judaism who were revered, who taught, who led. But they did not change the system, they were merely exceptions to it, as has been the case at most periods and in most places since.

The remarkable thing about what Jesus did was that he did not make exceptions to the system; rather he dismantled it. If we read the gospels in a superficial and traditional way we might suppose, given the small amount of space allotted to women, that we are indeed dealing with a few exceptions, and not very remarkable ones at that. It takes the kind of carefully imaginative awareness I have tried to use here, together with the fruits of much honest and detailed study by scholars of both sexes, to show that what Jesus did with and for women was at the very heart of his mission. The abolition of sexual roles in his entourage, and in the missionary generation immediately following, was not just one of a number of radical changes he made, rather it was the key one, the one which made possible all the rest.

This is so because women were the majority in the categories of people Jesus turned to as God's beloved. But they were not only the majority, they were in each case likely to be the most typical. Of the poor, now as then, most are women, and indeed the Torah constantly reminded believers of the plight of widows and orphans and commanded that they be cared for. Even when poor families are intact it is the women who carry the greatest burdens, literally as well as spiritually. Blessed are the poor.

Blessed also are the mourners, and they are women too, grieving for children who sicken and die from malnutrition or abuse, or grow up warped; grieving for men brutalized by want, grieving for girlhood abused and old age abandoned, grieving for husbands or brothers killed or crippled by dangerous work, work that weakens and demoralizes.

If those are to rejoice who are persecuted for faith we need to remember how the conversion of women to Christianity was perceived. It was bad enough for sons to leave home and follow Jesus, but when mothers and daughters and wives did so, the threat to the social order was mortal. We know from later stoies of martyrs what was done to some women who dared to defy the patriarchal system. The stories show that the refusal of the women, often scarcely more than children, to stick to their role, to marry as ordered, to sacrifice to their fathers' gods and keep the patriarchal home intact, provoked a savagery of punishment seldom aimed at male converts, even slaves. The women were not only challenging traditional religion, they were challenging the whole social system at its roots. The men could be punished as criminals, but the women's crime was deeper and provoked a degree of savage malice which betrays the fear behind it. If the women were from middle-class families, their behaviour challenged the very basis of their culture, which was the unquestioned right of the male to rule the household, to dispose of his possessions including children, slaves, and women, and to demand that all of them share his cult.

Blessed are the poor, the mourners, the hungry and thirsty for justice, those who have suffered injustice more than men because justice was not a concept intended to extend to them. Blessed are the meek, the powerless, the ones who are by definition without power because they belong to somebody, have no status of their own — the slaves, the women.

Shall the meek inherit the earth? Shall those who labor and are heavy-laden find relief, the carriers of babies and water pots, those who bear the burden of disappointment, abandonment, endless labor, who nurse the sick, support the aged?

At the heart of Jesus' summons to the poor and oppressed are the women. They are not alone, and they do no want to be alone or exclusive. Indeed the nature of their poverty and their suffering lies in their inextricable links to the poverty and suffering of others, of those they love as well as those they fear but from whom they cannot escape. The women are not a separate class of oppressed people, they *are* the oppressed, carrying the results of oppression in their hearts and hands, holding and upholding the oppressed, whether they like it or not.

We can see from this why the thing Jesus did for and with women is so central. It has been the hardest thing for the later followers of Christ to admit, in fact the vast majority never admitted it at all. The patriarchal order of the world (Judaic and Greco-Roman) in which Christianity emerged was only briefly disturbed by the teaching of Jesus in this area for the teaching shifted quietly. In some places, distrusted, slandered, and persecuted Christians wanted to prove they were not, as accusers said, disturbers of the peace, law-breakers. So Christian leaders demanded that wives and slaves of pagan men conform to the norms of the patriarchal household, thus proving that Christian wives and slaves could be as submissive and law-abiding as any; their religion was to be "within" and not rock the boat of a patriarchal state. But the expedient was soon adopted as normal for Christian households also, since that made it much easier for Christians to be accepted.

Pushing in the same direction, the fears of Christian men who felt their roles undermined helped to hasten the suppression of women. The only surprising thing is how long the resistance lasted. We can tell from the exhortations to submission in historical and other sources that women were not easily deprived of the freedom they had been given. Once more (at the risk of being boringly repetitious) it is essential to realize that the emancipation of women by Jesus was different; it was not an admission of some women into some male roles, as was not uncommon in both Jewish and Gentile society. It was much more radical. From the patriarchal point of view it was even worse in its effects than the cult of Isis and other religious movements which attracted women and slaves because they were given equal status as worshippers. Those movements abolished sex distinctions in the area of religion, and were dangerous because they broke the essential religious unity of the patriarchal household, but they did not alter the pattern of household authority. The Christian proclamation, in its early stages, did that. It changed the relationship within the family, it even liberated women and men *from* the family if necessary, giving them a new family of believers instead. It was the total abolition of role distinctions, it undermined the foundations of society, religiously and socially, and it could not be allowed to continue. But the virulence of the attacks on it show how difficult was the struggle to suppress it. It seems that it lasted longer in some churches than other, though after a while those churches which maintained it were labelled heretic by those which were rapidly establishing a power block of dominance and control.

The suppression, however, was never totally successful, and it is worthwhile to take a brief look at the underground movement of Christian women through the centuries. There are now many books celebrating these heroines, and this is merely a glance at the array. As we have seen, even in the curious language of "becoming male" Christians found themselves admitting that women and men could and did show equal courage and strength under persecution. Women in such circumstances could transcend the roles of motherhood and wifely or daughterly submission, and be approved for doing so.

With the rise of the ascetic tradition, there was another possibility for women: as virgins and ascetics they could escape the traditional roles, find freedom and respect as Christian persons in their own right. Wealthy women founded and led monastic communities, initiated charitable projects, founded hospitals, gathered other women to share this life work, to study Scripture, to pray. Even there they were often a source of anxiety to male ascetics who could not deal with their own sexuality, and the sad fact is that although we have plentiful writings of the desert fathers and other male spiritual writers and theologians of early centuries, the women were not allowed to write anything under their own name. Perhaps some did, and their work was destroyed. In any case, none has survived. Although their scholarship was known and attested, they could act only as aides to the men. Jerome might praise the wisdom and intelligence of his friend, Paula, and admit her

Hebrew to be better than his, but she could not write anything for others to read. The later women's monastic tradition, however, is the story of scientific and artistic achievement, of the creation of centers of "peace studies", of places where women could lead, share, pray, and grow as persons in their own right. (It is no coincidence that several of these monastic women have places at "The Dinner Party.)

In time, even this sphere of freedom for women became too much for a patriarchal church to cope with. The freedoms of women's monasteries were gradually but steadily reduced, cloister was stringently imposed (for women only), male clerics imposed to supervise the women. There were always individual exceptions, but exceptions they remained, and even these were often persecuted.

The Reformation did nothing to help either side. Catholic rules of cloister were tightened, so that when Louise de Marillac and her friend Vincent de Paul wanted their Daughters of Charity to be free to serve the poor wherever and however they were needed, they had to resort to the fiction that these girls were not really nuns. As they made yearly promises, not solemn vows, they could escape the cloister. Jeanne de Chantal's Visitation nuns, less cunning, were originally intended also to serve the sick in the cities, but were soon confined to cloister with the rest. As for the Protestant women, they lost even the small degree of choice offered by the religious life. They were subject to patriarchal household authority from cradle to grave. If Catholic nuns owed obedience always to some male cleric, Protestant wives were subject to their husbands in everything, as indeed were Catholic wives, though the severity of the rule varied. (Englishmen in the seventeenth century were reputed not to beat their wives very much.)

In some ways, however, the seventeenth century seems to have been the time of most complete suppression for Christian women, though on both sides there were exceptions. Many Protestant and Catholic women became known and revered in their time as mystics and leaders. But they remained exceptional, and even they generally accepted the sexual roles assigned by their church and society, seeking rather to stretch them than change them. One corporate exception was the Society of Friends, in which George Fox's meeting with, and later marriage to, Margaret Fell was crucial. Margaret's insight, unique as it was, found immediate echoes in the hearts of other women, and what she perceived is helpful to us now. The "Quakers", as they were called in derision because of their ecstatic type of prayer, refused any kind of cult or ritual, and therefore excluded cultic authority, which had traditionally been male; this made it easier for women to play a part. Their meetings were meetings of equals. But other sects embracing a non-ritualistic and spirit-guided life-style still preserved the patriarchal family structure, and this prevailed in worship also in many cases, though not all. The Quakers managed to keep the equality of the sexes as an unalterable part of their faith practice, though in time the submission of wives in the domestic sphere, as opposed to the religious sphere, became usual among the Quakers also. The reason for this clarity is to be found in the creative theological mind of Margaret Fell, which took the premises of the infant Society to their logical conclusion. Through her powerful leadership and her radical theology, the equality of the sexes founded on Scripture was built into the Society from the start. Her pamphlet on "Women's Speaking, Justified, Proved and Allowed by the Scriptures" dealt with the same issues, texts and incidents which feminist theologians are dealing with now. (It is subtitled: "And how WOMEN were the first that preached the tidings of the Resurrection of Jesus, and were sent by Christ's own command before he ascended to the Father"). It is interesting that in her exegesis of the Pauline command that women be silent in the church she uses the argument that the women forbidden to speak are those who have not received the spirit of prophecy, and are still "under the Law." This ingenious argument may not stand up to modern critical methods, but its importance lies in the fact that Margaret saw the equality of women as grounded in the acceptance of the gospel. Women and men became equals and co-workers in Christ; the Spirit set them free from "the Law", that is from the customs and laws of patriarchal society.

If this idea is followed through, it seems that Margaret is saying that the assumption of roles of prophecy, mission and leadership by women are the result of having been set free from bondage to sin, therefore from the domain of the Law. Those who continue to submit, and do not protest their oppression, are those still in bondage spiritually. The gospel proclamation of freedom of life, then, is not a proclamation of religious privilege for the believer, but of the fact that men and women are created equal, and only "sin" has brought about the subordination of one to the other. The good news is that people are capable of living as they were created to live.

The offshoot of the Quakers which flourished for over a hundred and fifty years in America was a group called "Shakers", and their contribution to feminist theology is important because equality of the sexes was a fundamental part of their way of life. Mother Ann, their foundress at the end of the eighteenth century, was understood to be the female Messiah, counterpart to the male Messiah, Jesus. God is Father/Mother, the Mother being Wisdom or Spirit. This theology, which saw masculine and feminine as aspects of deity was reflected in the equality of male and female in the Shaker communities. This was an hierarchical structure, but the hierarchy was paired between the sexes from top to bottom. Men and women lived in the same very large family homes, but were celibate, because it seemed to them that only celibacy could liberate from the forms of the unredeemed world. This was perfectly correct if we recognize that marriage and family inevitably meant the subordination of one sex to the other, and it is no wonder that many women joined the Shakers, leaving husbands or families because that highly disciplined life offered a sense of self-respect, a scope for creativity and leadership, which were unattainable elsewhere.

It is interesting that Shaker theology put enormous emphasis on the creation of beautiful as well as useful things. Radical simplicity was combined with a sensitive feeling for beauty of design, and nowadays thousands flock to admire the furniture and buildings they left. Original Shaker furniture is now precious, and vastly expensive, but reproductions continue to proliferate and give pleasure. The care of the Shakers for the earth, for natural and human-made beauty, their respect for the dignity of everyday life and things, are the result of a theology that grew from a "feminine" or "right brain" type of consciousness. For them, in their time, it was only within the circle of the redeemed, that little world they had created within their own areas of land and their own villages, that this harmony could reign and worldly division, oppression and exploitation be avoided. They had no missionary thrust, though they explained their ideas forcefully to visitors. They strove rather to maintain their way of life, which they believed was that of the resurrection, and allow it to grow. In this they were quite unlike the Quakers who had no separate areas nor closely structured community life, and at least in the early generations were strongly missionary.

In both cases it seems that the re-ordering of social relationships sprang from theological premises that perceived the equality of the sexes as integral not only to the gospel but to the nature of human beings and of God. But the Shakers' explicit affirmation of beauty and creativity in work and life was a further theological development of what was implied by the feminine consciousness of God: nurturance, not dominance, holistic development of resources rather than exploitation, was to be the Christian attitude to created beings. If the need to escape from the forms of the world imposed celibacy, Shaker women and men were extremely fertile in other ways, as had been the celibate monastic women and men before them.

The Shakers were direct successors of the Quakers, and indeed seventeenth century England burgeoned suddenly with radical sects, many of which explicitly gave women equality, and with that often enough the freedom to marry and divorce at choice, equally with men. The group called the Diggers which flourished briefly in the mid-seventeenth century was one such radical, pacifist, Christian community. They would not bear arms, claimed the earth as a common heritage for all, refused to pay rent or acknowledge rank, and proclaimed their right to "make the waste grounds grow" no matter who claimed to possess them. They did not survive for long the wrath of the landlords. Their gospel-based theology, with its emphasis on common use and life, is reminiscent of the Native American attitude to land and property, one shared by many "primitive" people, and although the Diggers did not give a prominent place to women their theology was linked to the holistic type of Christian theology which has emerged among women and men who are in touch with a feminine type of consciousness.

The feminine consciousness, and an explicitly feminine understanding of women's role, was part of the motivation of women in the large denominations in the nineteenth century, as well as in the "Holiness" movement and many sects. The remarkable work of many groups of women, Protestant and Catholic, in the time after the Industrial Revolution had less to do with any sense that sex roles should be redefined than with an energetic response to need. Because of what they did these women had to engage in a spirited defense of their activities as being within the appropriate sex roles. Groups of middle-class women who worked to help poor families, or "fallen" women, Catholic Sisters who ventured into industrial slums or Indian territories or new mining townships were not, on the whole, feminist, and grew very angry when accused of breaking out of the proper role for Christian women. They did not realize that, whatever they said, just by doing what they did — but most of all by organizing what they did for themselves — they were a threat to the established churches. The were alienated and hurt by the accusations of being "unfeminine" hurled at them by the clergy. Some capitulated and submitted to being helpers to male groups. Others held out and, by so doing became radicalized, for the actual experience of confronting the results of social policies framed entirely by men was itself a radicalizing process.

Women from the "sect" type of tradition also became politically aware when as Christians they began carrying into the political sphere their sense of themselves as equally called to preaching and church leadership One example of this has been the involvement of black Christian women in the civil rights movement, which they have seen as truly a biblical, Christian issue. It is interesting to see the ways in which women made the connection between their calling as Christians with a function in the religious sphere, and their right and duty to become politically active. To make connections between the gospel proclamation and the emancipation of any particular group of people it is not enough to suffer oppression; it has proved easy to persuade whole subject populations that their condition was God's will, that "spiritual" freedom, unaffected by exterior conditions, was what Jesus was talking about. That this has been possible, given his very explicit attitude to the rich and exploitative classes, remains amazing. Women have been vulnerable to religious language (the only kind available to them) which taught them to regard their bodies as, at best, a handicap in the race for salvation, and so persuaded them to seek to develop their spiritual selves by accepting humiliation and suffering as God-sent. For women to perceive themselves as unjustly oppressed they had to learn to question patriarchal assumptions which were part of their traditional and internalized way of thinking and feeling.

For women in some smaller sects and movements, this change was a development of their church experiences, though it has to be recognized that in the last century, as now, many fundamentalist groups have taught and imposed a violently sexist theology. For women from the larger denominations it was more difficult. The amazing thing is that so many, while accepting all the doctrines and superstructure of male hierarchical religion, discovered a strong relationship with God and confidence to follow a calling which cut across at least some patriarchal expectations. They did this out of that same sense of connectedness which we saw as characteristic of the relationship of women with Jesus, and with each other around him. Even the distorted nineteenth century mystique, by which women were taught to see themselves as saviours of society through their preservation of a domestic feminine sphere of compassion and purity untouched by the wicked commercial world of men, was expressing a sense of this interrelatedness. And when some broke out of this and carried the same ideals into the slums and brothels, or brought education and health care to the industrial poor, they acted in that same solidarity. If the spiritual language was inadequate, the actions and feelings were clear. They knew themselves called, and claimed the freedom to respond, and their calling was inseparable from the compassion they felt, the relationship they perceived with each other in a new way, and with the poor also.

Women, who are of the poor, who are of the "other", the vulnerable, are linked to all the vulnerable and easily exploited, linking all creation in fact and feeling. They are therefore essentially not a pressure group, or a special case; they are not separate at all. Unless they train themselves out of it for defense and survival, women are aware of the interdependence of human life and all life. They feel things bodily and feel the connections. The women who met Jesus and discovered a new life related to him directly as a physical, actual person. Children relate like this, and men and women continue to do so until they are taught not to. They are all taught not to, but for women the teaching is less intensive, it has holes in it, created by the expectation that motherhood, and other "feminine" experiences, will be important. The crippling toughness and individualism demanded of men is not expected of women to the same extent. As Marilyn Ferguson says in *The Aquarian Conspiracy*, "women have cultural permission to be more intuitive, sensitive, feeling. Their natural milieu has been complexity, change, nurturance, affiliation, a more fluid sense of time".

On the other hand the role models of excellence are mostly male, and women who want to excel look to them. One of the things Jesus did for women was to provide a role model which was undoubtedly male (and therefore acceptable to a society which, like ours, assumed that the male was the norm) but which was also obviously appropriate to their own sense of self and of life. It was a model of a nurturing person, compassionate and intuitive, but also that of a leader, an organizer, a person who could be assertive and take initiatives. The God who spoke in Jesus was a God they could relate to, and in whom they could relate to others. The men found it harder to find a role model in him, for this reason, and constantly tried to fit him into existing roles. It seems likely on the evidence that he felt much more comfortable with the women than with the men who so consistently misunderstood him.

It is clear that for much of Christian history this model has not been available, either to men or women. Something quite different has been substituted: a judge, a guru, a military leader, a passive sufferer, a gentle sympathizer, a youth counselor, a mystical lover or an unworldly dreamer. But if we are to suggest that Jesus provides a genuine and liberating model for women and men we have to provide some support for this interpretation. Since the other "Jesus's" have somehow also managed to support themselves on the gospels, how can the liberator of women, the angry and compassionate and needy leader, the ambivalent and reluctant messiah, the unalienated and vulnerable revolutionary, prove himself? To provide the answer to the question whether Jesus is indeed saviour, redeeming women and men from the rule of death, we need to recognize how Jesus identified himself, what kind of person he perceived himself to be. And the answer to that question brings us once more to the heart of the women's issue by another route, for the evidence of the New Testament is that Jesus thought of himself as the child of divine Wisdom, the feminine personification of God.

The "Wisdom" literature spans a period of about two hundred years at the end of the Old Testament period. It was a reaction of Jewish thought to exposure to Wisdom literature in impinging cultures, Egyptian and Mesopotamian. Much of it consists of very down-to-earth, not to say cynical, recommendations concerning desirable behaviour of men at court who want to get on well, and in this context it is openly mysogynist. It appeals to the situations of men whose religious tradition has lost the prophetic impulse and needs a rationale for accomodation to a state of affairs that seems unlikely to change. It was the work of scribes and professional "wise men" to whom the young should be attentive — and who were very clear that women were likely to distract the dedicated careerist and lead him into idleness and failure. Yet in all this comfortable and worldly pessimism there had to be some way to understand that God, after all, is present in human life and doings. The God here is not the energetic, revolutionary God of the Exodus and the prophets, yet there is need nonetheless to understand that God is at work in human life as it is experienced, and that somehow this is, truly, the God of Israel. In trying to do this the writers call on the imagery of the goddess cultures, for this is a God who is present in all creation, giving life and nurturing understanding. The creative power of this God works from within, imparting knowledge and insight, this God is companion, mother or sister. Divine Wisdom, the feminine Sophia, is the divine activity in goddess guise, and this is the personification of God on which Jesus calls to express his own sense of relationship to the people he loves. It is also to the Wisdom poetry that New Testament writers turn in their attempt to understand the role of Jesus as Christ, as sent forth from the Father.

Jesus was aware of the importance of the Wisdom tradition in his own time and of its ambivalence for his own purposes. He rejoiced that his Father had "hidden these things from the wise and prudent" and revealed them to little ones. But his poor and despised followers were the true family of Wisdom, who is "justified in all her children", because they show her influence and "upbringing" in their actions. In *Matthew* (11:25-30) the thanksgiving of Jesus for the gift of Wisdom to these "simple" or "little ones" is followed by the famous call quoted earlier: "Come to me, all whose work is hard, whose load is heavy, and I will give you relief, for my yoke is easy and my burden light." This is the Wisdom who reassures (*Eccles*. 51:23-27): "Come to me, you who need instruction — bend your neck to the yoke, be ready to accept discipline. See for yourselves how little were my labors compared with the great peace I have found." The wisdom gained by the discipline of the scribes is offered freely to the poor: for their heavy yoke ("you bind heavy burdens on men's shoulders") is substituted the "easy and light yoke and load" of Wisdom herself.

In John's gospel there is a deliberate attempt to associate the mission of divine Wisdom with the mission of Jesus. The theological construction of the passage is John's, but the words echo the tone and attitude of so much of the Synoptic account of Jesus that it is hard to refuse to recognize an authentic memory at the heart of it. In the *Ecclesiasticus*, Wisdom cries out, "Come to me, you who desire me, and eat your fill of my fruit — whoever feeds on me will be hungry for more, and whoever drinks from me will thirst for more". So in *John* it is the "child of Wisdom" who claims to fulfill what is promised: "Whoever comes to me shall never be hungry, whoever believes in me shall never be thirsty". Wisdom, and Wisdom's child, offer food, growth, life. Wisdom, in *Eccle-*

siasticus, is the one who led the people out of Egypt, fed them with manna, gave them water to drink, showed them the way. She says "I will water my garden," which is Israel, but the watercourse leading to the garden becomes a river, then a sea, and recalls the one who promised to give "living water", streams of water which flow from every person who believes.

There are few phrases from Wisdom poetry which can be attributed with a degree of certainity to Jesus himself, but the few are important and enable us to pick up the evidence of the tendency in Jesus to reflect Wisdom concepts, not only in words but in behaviour. In the experience of persecution both John the Baptist and Jesus stand in the succession of those prophets, some of them opposed and persecuted, whom Wisdom claims as her emissaries, accompanying and comforting them in prison and suffering. More subtly, it is the "personal" qualities of personified Wisdom which Jesus reflects. God as Wisdom is a nurturing, compassionate God, calling and yearning to her errant children, offering food and teaching: she "stands at the crossroads, by the wayside, at the top of the hill, beside the gate, at the entrance to the city, at the entry by the open gate she calls aloud" (*Prov.* 8:2-3). Unlike the official teachers who wait for their students to come to them, Wisdom, like Jesus, is out where the people are, waiting for them, calling to them, available and open to all. When Wisdom gives a feast she sends out "maidens" to summon her guests: the guests are the "simple", who are yet capable of Wisdom. Jesus, child and prophet of Wisdom, also summons one and all to his table.

There is something beyond this, however. If we can truly say that Jesus identified with the Wisdom expression of God then we are in touch with an experience of God which relates to the theme of this book in two ways. First, as I have already suggested, it presents God in a way which must have been both amazing and deeply satisfying to women, and explains to a great extent the enthusiasm and fidelity of their discipleship. Secondly, it bridges centuries by allowing us to recognize in the Wisdom-consciousness of Jesus and his women disciples that same new consciousness which is emerging in our time, that feminine type of consciousness which brings hope of unprecedented wholeness for the human race. But the panic drive to suppress it, the military build-up, the use of technology to dominate and exploit rather than to liberate, the escalating violence against the earth itself, show how fundamental in our culture — virtually any culture — is the fear of that other way of living, the way personified by divine Wisdom and lived out by Jesus and his friends. It is the same fear which fuelled the medieval witch-phobia, and which caused the vicious reaction to the suffragette movement. It is the fear which led to the suppression of women in Christianity so soon after its beginnings, yet the very strength of that fear shows how strong and fundamental is the power which it opposes, the power we can identify as that of divine Wisdom.

This is the power of life itself, present and active in all places, "making the circuit of the sky," and traversing "the depth of the abyss, through the waves of the sea" and in "every people and nation." This divine, pervasive presence is "all powerful, all surveying, and permeating all intelligent, pure and delicate spirits ... like a fine mist she rises from the power of God, a pure effluence of the glory of the Almighty. She is the reflection of everlasting light, flawless mirror of the active power of God and image of his goodness." Paul, writing to the Colossians, refers to the Christ as "image of the invisible God, his is the primacy over all created things", "in him him everything in heaven and on earth was created," for he is that Wisdom who, [in the Book of Wisdom] "is but one, yet can do everything, herself unchanging, she makes all things new." He is the one who in the words of the writer to the Hebrews is "the effulgence of God's splendor and the stamp of God's very being, and sustains the universe by his word of power." Wisdom, the God of Jesus, is a power that unites, that transforms, that inspires, moves, sustains, comforts, nourishes. She moves through all creation and is active not against, but within, human hearts and minds, "making them friends of God and prophets."

The description of Wisdom, and the self-description of Jesus, are the descriptions of the new consciousness in our time, which grows from the sense of the essential inter-dependence of all things, the awareness that the basic reality is one of flow, of exchange of being, of movement and energy which is transformative. The description of essential reality put forward by modern physicists come remarkably close to being poems of divine Wisdom.

The power of the new, right-brain, "feminine" consciousness is revolutionary. It calls for a rethinking of all aspects of life — education, economics, health, industry, agriculture — so that life may persist on earth. Where it is tried, it works, but it is hard to persuade people of patriarchal inclination even to try it. This is what Jesus found, when he called on people to realize the divine power which was theirs if only they would believe. Few did — yet the option remains open, at least for a while. When we get in touch with what happened to those women who followed Jesus, in his earthly lifetime and later, we find that the attitude of Jesus to women, and their response to that, is at the heart of his promise of liberation for the whole creation. Because of the refusal of the Christian church to follow him in this, his mission has not been carried out, except here and there in patches. The transformative power evoked in the Wisdom literature and incarnate in Jesus is the hope of the world, and it is available, not just among Christians but wherever human beings allow themselves to be aware of the divine power bursting through the ground like shoots in spring. This is Wisdom, crying at the gates, weeping in compassion, entering into hearts and minds to break down barriers and transcend categories. Her fruits are those outbreaks of joy, friendship, energy, creative action, which happen among people who are open to belief in the goodness of the reality at the heart of things.

The new consciousness is aware of the redefinition of power which Jesus brought. More women are realizing that the thrust of early feminism to take over the male roles was inadequate; political and social equality matter, but to compete in the male power games is not the answer. Women are not now asking for a piece of the patriarchal pie; they want to bake a different one. Many women are afraid of power because to them power means control and oppression, but they — and men also — are learning that power can be a liberating and uniting force, that empowerment is for relatedness, love, hope. Leadership need not mean dominance, though women "in power" too often assume this. There is an alternative, and the leadership of many women in the past, and many men too, has taken its character from the leadership to which Jesus called women and men; a leadership which listens, calls, encourages, which inspires confidence, relies on the goodness of each and affirms the dignity of the least. From such leadership the skills of consensus can grow, people can liberate one another and work together for the common goals.

An often-noticed phenomenon of the Christian scene at present is that wherever the liberating power of the gospel is most clearly at work, there women predominate. There are more of them, and they tend to be in leadership roles. They work comfortably with men, but for the men sensitive enough and strong enough to respond to this situation, such collaboration is not easy. In a society characterized by male violence against women and denigration of women at every level it is hard for such men to discover an appropriate male role. Many are seeking it, and their courage and goodness carry hope. They know, and the women know, that in their sharing of mission they are empowering the "little ones" and carrying the hope of a new future.

There is one symbol which, through the centuries, has carried the meaning of feminine being and power, and at the end of this book it becomes significant. The symbol of the Grail begins with the pagan stories of a cauldron of plenty, a magical dish or cup that brings food to those who wait for it. Sometimes it is a stone, a jewel of transformation. It is hidden from all but those enlightened. It became associated with the cup of the Last Supper of Jesus, the receptacle of his blood, and in some stories it caught drops of his blood as he hung on the cross. It is carried across the sea, kept in a magical castle, guarded by knights and wise maidens. It is sought by many and seen by few. To gaze into it is to perceive the ultimate mysteries, but only those with pure hearts attain to it.

The Grail is closely linked to the myths around Mary, mother of Jesus. She is hailed as "Ark of the Covenant" in which God rested; "Seat of Wisdom", for Wisdom sat in her lap; "vessel of honor", "spiritual vessel", which contained the "spiritual drink" of salvation. The goddess-symbol of Mary and the goddess-symbol of Wisdom come together in the symbol of the vessel in which life, wisdom and the secrets of salvation, are to be found.

The Christ pours his blood into this vessel, and it is guarded by wise women. It is the symbol of the feminine as life-giver, that which was evoked powerfully in the image of "The Dinner Party" itself — a "Last Supper", a eucharistic banquet of women. The central symbol of that modern art form is the womb, the place of life, and that is also the meaning of the Grail, and the power of the image of Mary. Symbols are always ambivalent and complex, but these converging images point us to a very simple and basic reality of women's experience, which is at the heart of their oppression and of their power: women can bear children, they can be mothers. Whether they actually bear children or not, the race depends on them, they are necessary. Hence the fear, the superstition, the creation of all the negative images of woman — woman as witch, goddess of death and darkness, devourer. Women hold the ultimate power and it cannot be taken from them.

This is something the women's movement has had trouble dealing with, because motherhood has traditionally been used as a means of keeping women "in their place". The capacity for motherhood is the source of women's power but also of their vulnerability. A woman can bear children, but she can also be raped. It is this very combination of power and vulnerability that Jesus called on in the women he encountered. Most of them were mothers, yet in his eyes they were not determined by their motherhood, neither were they required to reject it. In their experience of being capable of motherhood these women discovered the power to use the qualities of motherhood in mission. They could do this because they saw Jesus, child of divine Wisdom, Grail King, doing just that. Ancient images speak of the dying Christ giving birth on the cross to a new people. The blood which the legends saw dripping into the Grail was recognized as the blood of birth. The women at the cross and the tomb shared in that birthing, bearing in their bodies the experience they could not understand or express.

Women, now, need to rediscover the power of motherhood, and to claim it as a liberating power. Whether or not they bear children in their bodies they are called to bear a new world to birth, if there is to be one at all. As we reflect on the needs of a world in the process of destruction we recognize that the qualities needed to save and heal the people and to nurture a different future are qualities of compassion, thoughful remembering, acute awareness and insight, directed by intelligent courage. There are the qualities of good nurturance. We recognize those qualities in Jesus, and percieve that he both responded to and called forth those qualities in the women who followed him, affirming and transforming them into a power of liberation and hope. The pain they experienced is the pain of all women who struggle to recognize and respond to Holy Wisdom in themselves. Not the least part of that pain is the knowledge that the ears of many women have been so dulled by the din of a blindly clamoring world that they cannot hear the sounds of a different song. That also was the pain of Jesus, as he found himself surrounded by those, men and women, who heard his words but could not hear his message, and so remained bound in a slavery they did not recognize. It was, in the end, through a death he could not evade without betraying the mission of divine Wisdom that the transforming power broke through. The history of women has been a way of the cross, lightened by moments of glory, glimpses of transfigured humanity on the mountain top. Through the centuries the power has been at work, laboring like Wisdom in secret ways, inspiring, calling, refusing to allow full play to the forces of destruction, yet refusing to fight them with their own weapons.

The symbol of the Grail draws it all together. It is the source of plenty, the nurturing power of the goddess; it contains the blood of willing sacrifice which is also the symbol of birth; it is the place of vision, and the source of power, but a power that liberates and transforms, the empowerment of those who have learned to see.